VEGETARI
FROM

By

AROONA REEJHSINGHANI

JAICO PUBLISHING HOUSE
Mumbai ● Delhi ● Bangalore
Calcutta ● Hyderabad ● Chennai

VEGETARIAN WONDERS FROM GUJARAT
ISBN 81-7224-274-3

First Jaico Impression: 1975
Eleventh Jaico Impression: 1999

Published by:
Ashwin J. Shah
Jaico Publishing House
121, M.G. Road
Mumbai - 400 001.

Printed by:
R.N. Kothari
Sanman & Co.
113, Shiv-Shakti Ind. Estate
Andheri (E), Mumbai - 400 059.

ABOUT THE AUTHORESS

Aroona Reejhsinghani is the only authoress today who has written more than 100 books on a single subject of cooking. She has written on every type of cooking, both Indian and International cooking. Her books have gone into many editions and are today selling throughout the world. Because of this singular achievement in 1991 she entered the Limca book records, she also entered the American book of honour and she was also congratulated by guiness book of world records for this singular achievement. She was for sometime editor-in-chief of Cuisine magazine India's first magazine on food, then she started her own magazine on Food "Aroona's world of food". Today she runs her own food consultancy service, she is recipe consultant to restaurants, sells her own creations like spices and pickles, does food styling and has worked for more than 30 multinationals for whom she creates new recipes and advises them on their products, she has also done signature modelling. This year she has been nominated by American Biographical Institute, North Caroline USA for the 2000 Millennium Medal of Honour a 24 ct. gold medal which is being bestowed upon select men and women around the world for extraordinary achievement during the last 100 years.

CONTENTS

				Pages
Introduction	...	...	...	1
Glossary	...	...	...	3
A few simple cooking terms	...	...	5
Household Hints	...	...	...	8
Dishwashing	...	...	...	10

Raitas

Chilli raita	...	...	...	...	17
Banana raita	...	...	...	...	17
Brinjal raita	...	...	...	...	17
Boondi raita	...	...	...	...	18
Doodhi raita	...	...	...	...	18
Cabbage raita	...	...	...	...	19
Cucumber raita	...	...	...	19
Suran raita	...	...	...	...	20
Bhopla raita	...	...	...	...	20
Raita of curry leaves	...	...	...	20
Mixed vegetable raita	...	...	...	21
Corn raita	...	...	...	...	21
Pudina raita	...	...	...	...	22
Khajur raita	...	...	...	...	22
Dhokli raita	...	...	...	...	22

Rice

Masala pullao	...	...	...	...	27
Sweet pullao	...	...	...	...	27
Biraj	...	...	...	...	28

Pages

Khichadi	28
Potato pullao	29
Vegetable pullao	30
Dal pullao	31
Onion pullao	32
Coconut biraj	32
Badshahi pullao	33
Dahi-dudh nu pullao	34

Sweets & Desserts

Mohanthal	39
Kaju pak	39
Copra pak	40
Badam pak	40
Corn pak	41
Gaunder pak	42
Poha pak	42
Kola pak	43
Sukri	43
Gol papadi	44
Dudhpak	44
Chickoo ka dudhpak	45
Basundi	45
Puran poli	46
Khoya poli	46
Flour sheera	47
Corn sheera	47
Dal sheera	47
Magaz	48
Malpura	48
Lapsi	49
Chickoo pak	49

Pages

Dahi pak 50
Kansar 50
Gheun ka dudhpak 51
Shrikhand 51

Puries, Theplas and Rotlies

Methi puri 55
Jeera puri 55
Masala puri 55
Mithi puri 56
Dahi puri 56
Vegetable puri 57
Potato puri 57
Bhakri 57
Puffed chapati 58
Thepla of methi 58
Mulanu thepla 59
Dal nu thepla 59
Moong and potato rotla 59
Batata nu rotla 60
Dal nu rotla 60
Vegetable rotla 61
Batatanu bhakri 61
Bajra rotli 62
Methi and bajra rotli 62

Pickles & Chutneys

Hot mango pickle 67
Spicy mango pickle 67
Mango and vegetable pickle 68
Chundo No. 1 68

Pages

Chundo No. 2 69
Red capsicum pickle 69
Lime pickle 69
Chilli pickle 70
Amla murraba 70
Amla ka chunda 71
Gaurkerry 71
Chilli chutney 71
Gram chutney 72
Corriander chutney 72
Peanut chutney 72
Sweet chutney 73
Coconut chutney No. 1 73
Coconut chutney No. 2 73
Onion chutney 74
Garlic chutney 74
Raisin chutney 74
Til chutney 74

Farshan

Dry fruit kachori 77
Peas kachori 77
Corn kachori 78
Potato kachori 78
Dal kachori 79
Sweet potato kachori 80
Aluvadi 80
Tomato omellete 81
Masala tikki 82
Dahi vada 83
Chutney vada 83
Urad dal bajia 84

Pages

Channa dal bajia 85
Vegetable vada 85
Dal handva 86
Vegetable handva 87
Doodhi handva 87
Cauliflower handva 88
Papaya tikki 88
Cabbage tikki 89
Dal tikki 90
Corn tikki 90
Corn rolls 91
Khakhada 92
Green channa chivda 92
Potato chivda 93
Corn chivda 93
Fried dal 94

Vegetables

Dudhi muthia 97
Muli muthia 97
Cabbage muthia 98
Methi muthia 98
Undhia 99
Potato dhokli 100
Gavar dhokli 101
Rice dhokli 102
Sago khichadi 103
Batata poha 103
Sabudana and potato khichadi ... 104
Shingh poha 104
Stuffed karela 105
Batata vangi nu shak 105

Pages

Brinjals fried	106
Stuffed brinjals	106
Stuffed capsicums	107
Corn in curds	107
Makka nu shak	108
Stuffed chillies	108
Mirchi nu shak	109
Kobi nu shak	110
Kachi kerry nu shak	110
Pukki kerry nu shak No. 1	111
Pukki kerry nu shak No. 2	111
Padval ka ravaiya	111
Padval nu shak	112
Papadi nu shak	113
Makkai ni khichadi	113
Batata ne tomato	114
Sweet and sour potatoes	114
Fried potatoes	115
Crunchy potatoes	115
Batata nu shak	116
Batata masala shak	116
Potatoes in curds	117
Masala ma batata	118
Suran Khichadi	118
Sweet potato dabada	119
Tomato shak	119
Tomato dabada	120

Curries

Bhindani curry	123
Corn curry	123
Doodhi kofta curry	124

Pages

Brinjal curry 125
Buttermilk curry 125
Mukund curry 126
Potato kofta curry 126
Tomato curry 128

Dals

Mixed dal 131
Radish in dal 131
Vegetable dal ...., ... 132
Pumpkin dal 133
Dal with sweet potatoes ... ..., 133
Dal moong 134
Dal toovar 135
Toovar dal No. 2 135
Sukhe val 136
Savoury peas 136
Dal with spinach 137
Toovar dal treat 138
Dal kofta curry 139
Moong curry 140

INTRODUCTION

Gujarat is perhaps the only vegetarian state in India for Gujaratis of all castes and creeds are staunch vegetarians. Certain ingredients like curds, buttermilk, coconut, groundnuts, sesame seeds, sugar and lime juice dominate Gujarati Food and the majority of the dishes contain one or more of these ingredients therefore Gujarati cuisine is considered a healthy one because it has so many protein-packed items of food as its base. The Gujaratis are very fond of snacks which in Gujarat are known as "Farshan". These are prepared in many different ways and are really very tasty. The best known Farshan is the Chivda which is made in dozen different ways with varying ingredients, after you have tasted it you will know why it has gained so much popularity in all the states of India. Gujarati's use sugar and lime juice in almost every dish which gives Gujarati food a unique sweet and sour taste which might not appeal to all people, but their Farshan, sweetmeats and specially pickles are unusually good. Gujarati pickles are perhaps the best pickles in India today and like chivda they too are slowly gaining popularity with all sections of people. Farshan, sweet-meats and pickles will become your favourites for all times to come if tried just once. All the recipes in this book are tried and tested, authentic and original and belong exclusively to Gujarat. I thank Mrs. Padmabahen Mehta, Vasubahen Shah and Mrs. Sonavaria for giving me their favourite recipes to include in this book.

AROONA REEJHSINGHANI

Glossary

English	Hindi	Gujerati
Ashgourd	Kashiphul	Kola
Bittergourd	Karela	Karela
Banana	Kela	Kela
Brinjal	Baigan	Vagan
Carrots	Gajjar	Gajjar
Corn	Makkai	Makkai
Cauliflower	Phoolgobi	Kobi flower
Cabbage	Bund gobi	Kobi
Collocasia leaves	Arbi ke patte	Aruniganth
Cucumber	Kheera	Kakadi
Cluster beans	Gavar	Gavarshingh
Drumstick	Shingh ki phaliyan	Sangveni shingh
Green onions	Hare pyaj	Nila kanda
Green peas	Mutter	Vatana
Ladies fingers	Bhendi	Bhinda
Mango	aamb	Keri
Onions	pyaj	Kanda
Pumpkin	Kadu	doodhi
Potatoes	Alu	Batata
Radish	muli	Mula
Sweet potato	Shakurkund	Shakariya
Yam	Zamin kand	Suran

Herbs and spices

English	Hindi	Gujerati
Asafoetida	hing	hing
Bay leaves	tejpatta	tejpatta
Corriander leaves	Dhania	Kothmer
Curry leaves	gandhela	Mitho-limbdo
Red Chillies	lal mirchi	Lal mircha
Corriander seeds	Sukha-dhania	Dhana
Cumin seeds	jeera	Jeeru
Caraway seeds	Shahjeera	Kali jeeru
Cinnamon	dalchini	Dalchini
Cardamoms	elachi	Elchi
Cloves	Lavang	Laving
Garlic	Lasun	Lasun
Ginger	Adhruk	Adhu.
Dry ginger	Saonth	Sunt

Fenugreek seeds	Methi	Methi
Jaggery	Gur	Gur
Mint	Paudina	Fudina
Mustard seeds	Rai	Rai
Poppy seeds	Khus-khus	Khus-khus
Peppercorns	Kali mirchi	Kali miri
Tamarind	Imli	Amli
Turmeric	Huldi	Hurdur
Sugar	Shakur	Shakur
Salt	Namak	Mithoo
Sesame seeds	Til	Tul
Saffron	Keshar	Kesar
Vinegar	Sirka	Surko

Nuts

Almonds	Badam	Badam
Cashewnuts	Kaju	Kaju
Dry coconut	Copra	Copra
Coconut	Narial	Narial
Dates	Khajur	Khajur
Pistachio nuts	Pista	Pista
Peanuts or groundnuts	Moongfali	Mandvi shingh
Raisins	Kishmish	Draksh

Lentils & flours

Bengal gram	Channe ki dal	Channa ni dal
Black gram	Urad ki dal	Urad ni dal
Beaten rice	Cheura	Poha
Green gram	Moong ki dal	Mug ni dal
Gram flour	Besun	Channa no lot
Refined flour	Maida	Maido
Red grams	Masur ki dal	Masur ni dal
Tur grams	Toovar ki dal	Tur ni dal
Semolina	Suji	Suji
Vermecelli	Seviyan	Seviyan

A Few Simple Cooking Terms

Beat......to beat with a rotary beater, fork or spoon any liquid or semi-liquid food with the express purpose of mixing the food thoroughly and making it smooth.

Blend......to combine several ingredients together.

Boil......to heat a mixture or a liquid until bubbles appear on the surface and vapour starts rising, also to continue the process thereafter.

Boiling point......the temperature at which a liquid begins to bubble around the edges.

Blanch......the food which is to be blanched should be covered with cold water, the water should be brought to a rolling boil and kept at the boiling temperature until the skin of the food which is being blanched begins to wrinkle. The vessel should be immediately removed from fire and the food should be drained thoroughly and it should be covered with cold water and the peel should be removed with fingers.

Batter......a mixture of flour and liquid. The consistency of batter is such that it can be stirred with a spoon and is thin enough to drop from a spoon.

Chill......to cool food by placing over ice or in the fridge.

Chop......to cut food into small pieces.

Combine......to mix two or more ingredients together.

Dice......to cut food into small pieces of uniform shape and size.

Dissolve......to melt.

Drain......to free a food from a liquid.

Deep fry......to fry in plenty of boiling ghee or oil.

Dough......is a mixture of flour and liquid. A dough is thick enough to knead or roll but it too stiff to stir or pour.

Garnish......to decorate food.

Grate......to rub food into small pieces on a grater.

Grind......to reduce food to a paste.

Gravy......liquid in which the food is cooking.

Knead......to work dough of any other food with hands till it turns smooth.

Melt......to melt until the ingredients are changed from solid to liquid.

Mince......to chop food as finely as possible.

Mix......to blend different ingredients together.

Parboil......to cook food partially in water.

Pare......to remove skin or peels of vegetables and fruits.

Roll...to place a ball of dough on a flat wooden board and roll out into any shape you like with help of a rolling pin.

Simmer......to cook over a low heat just below the boiling point.

Shred......to reduce the food into small, long and narrow pieces.

Squeeze......to drain out all the liquid from a food by crushing or pressing it between your hands.

Soak......to cover food with water until wet.

Stalk, sprig or a flake......an individual piece either in corriander or garlic. For example the various sprigs of corriander make up a bunch of corriander leaves and the various flakes of garlic make up a whole pod of garlic.

Shallow fry......to fry in little ghee or oil In shallow frying the oil should just coat the bottom of the pan.

Steam......to cook food by contact with live steam in a covered or a perforated container placed over hot water.

House-hold Hints

1. To prepare a bowl of solid and thick curds, mix a teaspoon of curds in a big cup of warmed milk, put in a bowl, cover the bowl and place either in a tin containing rice or wheat for about 6 hours at the end of which you will have lovely solid curds before you.

2. To make curds at home without the aid of marketed curds. Boil 2 cups of milk, cool till warm and put in a few pods of tamarind. Cover and set the bowl in a warm place for 24 hours at the end of which you will find that the milk has turned solid. Remove the tamarind and mix in another 2 cups of warm milk. Cover the bowl again and set aside for another 24 hours. The curds will then be fit for use and can also be used for preparing fresh curds.

3. To preserve wheat and rice put in the containers red chillies and neem leaves.

4. Always eat the fried things like the bajias and cutlets immediately. If you can not eat them immediately then store them uncovered for if you will cover them they will turn soft because then the steam will not be able to escape from them. As long as steam keeps escaping from them they remain crisp, but once steam stops escaping they turn soft and soggy.

5. To preserve pure ghee put a leaf of turmeric

in it. It will not only preserve it but will also give it a lovely colour, taste and smell.

6. To improve rancid butter for every 125 grams of rancid butter take ¼ cup of fresh milk. Warm the butter slightly but do not melt it. Beat the butter nicely with a pinch of salt. Then go on beating in a little milk at a time till the butter will not absorb any more. Stand in the fridge or over ice or till the butter turns solid and you will have good solid butter to enjoy again.

7. To shorten cooking time of pulses like kabuli channa, red beans etc. soak them whole night in water to which a big pinch of soda bicarbonate has been added, then boil in plain water.

8. Soak walnuts in water for 1 week changing water every day. After a week shell and eat them and they will taste sweet and delicious and as fresh as though they were just then plucked from a tree. They last for a week in a cool, dry place or if kept in the fridge.

9. To remove bitterness from gourds, peel and rub on them mixture of flour, salt and water. Set aside for 1 hour and then wash them nicely in water before using them in any called for recipe.

10. If you want to extract extra juice from limes squeeze out the juice from the limes, set them aside for 15 minutes and then squeeze them once more. This way you will get a lot of extra juice.

Dish Washing

The main purpose of dish washing is to clean and to sanitise the dishes and utensils. The pots and pans soiled in the process of cooking should be very thoroughly scraped with a nylon scourer and then they should be soaked in hot water. After that put them one by one in hot, boiling water and leave them in it for half a minute so that all the bacteria which are on the surface of these dishes are killed. This is known as sanitizing the vessels which eliminates the health hazards. Now lift out the vessels one by one from the water and place them on the draining board so that they dry in the air, they should be then stacked on the racks or hung from hooks. But if your pots and pans happen to be very greasy then for each pan take one peel of sour lime, 1 tsp. salt and 1 cup hot water and put the ingredients in the pan. Bring the mixture to a boil, cool and then rub the sides of the pan with the peel for a few minutes. Throw away the mixture then wipe the pan with a rag. Now repeat the dish-washing procedure. If any of your vessels have got burnt then the best remedy is to fill them with salt water solution and leave them overnight. Next morning, bring the water to a boil, cool and then follow the dish-washing procedure. In case the burns are stubborn then rub the burnt areas with a mixture of salt, soda bicarbonate and lime juice. You can clean all types of utensils by following the procedure given above, but to get the best results there are different ways of cleaning utensils of different materials and if you will follow the instructions given below, your vessels will always sparkle and shine and look as good as new.

Aluminium vessels......should be cleansed in hot soapy water after each use. Rinse them in hot water dry them thoroughly before putting them away. Aluminium vessels often become discoloured. This is harmless and will not affect the food. To dissolve this discolouration scrub it nicely with a piece of coconut fibre dipped in coal ashes. Wash the vessel nicely and then put in equal quantities of hot water and lime juice and boil the solution in the discoloured pan for 5 minutes. Then follow the dishwashing procedure.

Tin Vessels......clean them with hot soapy water using a nylon scourer. To remove grease from these vessels soak them in boiling water in which one tablespoon of soda has been added. Leave for half an hour then wash in the usual way. To make these utensils rust-proof, rub them nicely with grease inside out and heat them in a moderate oven for half an hour. Remove cool, wash and then use them.

Iron Vessels......to remove a heavy coating of grease from these utensils boil them in a strong solution of soda bicarbonate and water. Remove from fire and then scour with a nylon scourer dipped in soap flakes. Then follow the dishwashing procedure. If your iron vessels have turned rusty you needn't worry.   Here is a safe and sure way of cleaning them of rust.   Rub the rusty vessel with coconut fibre dipped in kerosine oil.   Wash it in plenty of hot soapy water wipe dry and then rub the utensil and its lid with any grease like oil or ghee and place in a warm oven for 3 to 4 hours.   Let the utensil cool with the grease still on and then follow the dishwashing procedure.   To make these utensils rust-proof follow the procedure of tin vessels.

Stainless steel utensils......clean these utensils with equal quantities of coal ashes and flour. This will not only remove grease but will also make them sparkle at the same time.   Never use any scourer on the vessels as this will scratch their surface leaving unsightly marks on them.

Glass utensils......wash in hot soapy water to which a pinch of washing blue has been added. This will give a sparkle to your glass-ware. Wash cut glass with warm soapy water with a soft brush.   If your cut glass is badly stained, soak the pieces overnight in hot soapy water to which a few drops of liquid ammonia has been added. Next morning wash in the usual way.

Chinaware utensils......clean in hot soapy water. To remove tea or coffee stains from your cups and teapots, rub them with salt mixed with lime juice and then wash in the usual way.   Wash gilted china in plain hot water in order to preserve the brightness of its decorative gold work. To remove tea and coffee stains from delicate china, rub with soft cloth dipped in soda bicarbonate and then wash immediately.

Silver vessels......make a paste of fine rangoli powder and water and apply nicely on these vessels. Set aside for half an hour then rinse them in water and wipe dry with a soft cloth. Another way of washing them is to soak them half an hour in a strong solution of soda bicarbonate and hot water, then wash in the usual way and wipe dry with a soft towel.

Brass vessels......cover them with thick tamarind juice and then rub them nicely with coconut fibre dipped in coal ashes or fine sand. Wash them thoroughly in plenty of water. Dry in the air as wiping with a cloth will leave marks upon them.

Copper vessels......wash with a strong solution of soda and water and then rinse in clear water. When this metal is exposed to acids verdigris forms on it. To get rid of this rub with a paste of fine rangoli powder and water and then follow the dishwashing procedure. Copper and brass vessels should be tinned regularly otherwise some of the metal may dissolve and affect food cooked in them.

Enamel vessels......clean the usual way but to remove the hard sediment from these vessels fill them with water to which some lime juice and soda bicarbonate has been added. Boil for 5 minutes and then follow the dishwashing procedure. These vessels should not be scoured as this will remove the surface glaze and darken them. If they become badly discoloured then rub them with baking soda and follow the dish-washing procedure. To prevent hard sediment from forming in a kettle keep a china marble or a broken piece of china constantly in it.

Earthenware vessels.....wash them in hot soapy water. Burnt food sticking to these dishes can easily be removed by rubbing them gently with a piece of damp cloth dipped in fine salt.

To clean a thermos flask, put in 2 tblsps. vinegar, $\frac{1}{4}$ cup of water and crushed egg shell. Shake well, leave it for 15 minutes, shake once again and a rinse. Now pour in hot water mixed with 2 tblsps. of soda bicarbonate. Set aside whole night. Next morning, rinse it well before using.

To clean sieves and graters, remove all food with a stiff brush. Rinse under running water and then wash in warm soapy water. Rinse once again under running water and then leave to dry.

The best way to clean an egg beater is to use an old toothbrush dipped in hot soapy water.

Clean girdles with soap flakes and washing soda using a small smooth stone and coconut fibre to rub. Rinse thoroughly and wipe dry.

Clean glass bottles by a few rice grains, lime juice and hot water. Shake for a few minutes and then rinse in clean water.

RAITA

Chilli Raita

100 grams chillies. 2 tblsps. finely grated coconut. 1 cup beaten curds. ¼ tsp. mustard seeds. A pinch asafoetida. A few sprigs of corriander leaves. 1 tsp. sugar. Salt to taste. ¼ tsp. turmeric powder.

Slit green chillies and remove the inner seeds. Heat 1 tblsp. ghee and add asafoetida and mustard seeds. When the seeds stop popping, put in turmeric, fry briefly, add chillies and fry till they start changing colour. Put 1 tblsp. water on top. Cover tightly and cook till soft. Put in the rest of the above ingredients with the exception of corriander leaves. Cook for 2 minutes and remove from fire. Serve when cold decorated with corriander leaves.

Banana Raita

2 ripe bananas, peeled and cut into thin rings. 2 cups beaten curds. 1 tsp. mustard seeds. A few mint leaves. Handful of corriander leaves 1-inch piece ginger, minced. A pinch asafoetida. 1 tsp. sugar. Salt and chilli powder to taste.

Grind the mustard to fine powder. Mix together all the above ingredients with the exception of green leaves. Serve decorated with green leaves.

Brinjal Raita

1 medium brinjal. 2 cup beaten curds. A few sprigs corriander leaves. 1 tsp. cumin seeds. 2 green chillies. 2 flakes garlic. 1-inch piece ginger. Salt and chilli powder to taste.

Hold brinjal over fire and roast till its skin wrinkles and turns black, toss in cold water.

peel and grind to a paste. Also grind cumin seeds, garlic and ginger and mix into curds along with ground brinjals, salt and chilli powder. Serve decorated with sprigs of corriander leaves.

Boondi Raita

50 grams gram flour. 1 tsp. each of chilli powder and ground cumin seeds. 200 grams beaten curds. 1 tsp. roasted and powdered cumin seeds $\frac{1}{2}$ tsp. garam masala. $\frac{1}{4}$ tsp. ground mustard seeds. A few sprigs corriander leaves. Salt and chilli powder to taste.

Mix together gram flour, chilli powder, salt and ground cumin seeds a pinch of soda bicarb along with enough water to form a thick batter. Heat enough ghee for deep frying to smoking, pour batter through a colander or bundi jara and fry till crisp. Remove and drain. Put bundi in hot water and take out immediately and squeeze out all the moisture Put the bundi into curds with all the above ingredients with the exception of roasted cumin seeds, garam masala, chilli powder and corriander leaves. Mix the curds well and sprinkle on top the remaining ingredients before serving.

Doodhi Raita

2 cups beaten curds. 100 grams doodhi or pumpkin, peeled and finely grated. 1 tsp. roasted and powdered cumin seeds. 1 tblsp. sugar. 1 tblsp. charoli. 1-inch piece ginger, minced. 1 tblsp. raisins. $\frac{1}{2}$ tsp. garam masala. A few sprigs corriander leaves. Salt and chilli powder to taste.

Steam the vegetable and squeeze out all the moisture. Mix into the curds with the rest of the above ingredients with the exception of raisins charoli and corriander leaves. Sprinkle the remaining ingredients on top before serving.

Cabbage Raita

2 cups beaten curds. A few inner heart leaves of cabbage, shreded finely. 1 tsp. roasted and powdered cumin seeds. 2 green chillies, minced. 1-inch piece ginger, minced. 1 tsp. sugar. A few sprigs corriander leaves. Salt and chilli powder to taste.

Mix together all the above ingredients with the exception of corriander leaves. Serve decorated with corriander leaves.

Cucumber Raita

2 cups beaten curds. 3 tender cucumbers, washed and grated finely. 1 tsp. dry ginger powder. 1 tsp. roasted and ground cumin seeds. A pinch of asafoetida. 1 tsp. sugar. $\frac{1}{4}$ tsp. mustard seeds. $\frac{1}{4}$ tsp. garam masala. A few sprigs corriander leaves. A few mint leaves. Salt and chilli powder to taste.

Mix together all the above ingredients with the exception of mustard asafoetida and green leaves. Heat 1 tsp. oil and toss in asafoetida and mustard seeds. When the seeds stop spluttering mix into the raita. Serve decorated with green leaves.

Suran Raita

2 cups beaten curds. 100 grams boiled suran or jami kand. 1 tsp. sugar. A few sprigs corriander leaves. ½ tsp. mustard seeds. Salt and chilli powder to taste.

Mash the suran to a paste and mix with all the above ingredients with the exception of mustard seeds and corriander leaves. Heat 1 tsp. oil and toss in the mustard. When they stop popping, put over the raita. Decorate with corriander before serving.

Bhopla Raita

2 cups beaten curds. 100 grams red bhopla, peeled and grated. 1 tsp. cumin seeds. 1 tsp. sugar. A few sprigs corriander leaves. Salt and chilli powder to taste. ¼ tsp. garam masala.

Steam the bhopla and squeeze out all the moisture. Mix together all the above ingredients with the exception of chilli powder, corriander leaves, and cumin seeds. Heat 1 tsp. of cumin seeds and toss in the cumin seeds, when they stop spluttering, mix into the raita. Sprinkle chilli powder on top and decorate with corriander leaves before serving.

Raita of Curry Leaves

1 cup beaten curds. 15 curry leaves. 4 green chillies. 1 tsp. cumin seeds. ¼ tsp. mustard seeds. Salt and chilli powder to taste. A pinch asafoetida. 1 tsp. sugar.

Fry the curry leaves till red and crisp in a little ghee. Roast cumin seeds: Grind cumin seeds, curry leaves and chillies to a paste and mix into the curds along with the rest of the above ingredients with the exception of asafoetida and mustard seeds. Heat 1 tsp. oil and toss in asafoetida and mustard. When the seeds stop popping, put over the raita and serve.

Mixed Vegetable Raita

2 cups beaten curds. 1 small firm tomato. 1 tiny onion. 1 small tender carrot. 1 small cucumber. 2 tblsps. peeled and shreded raw beetroot. 2 green chillies, minced. Handful of sliced corriander leaves. A few sliced mint leaves. ½ tsp. dry ginger powder. 1 tsp. roasted and ground cumin seeds. 1 tsp. sugar. Salt and chilli powder to taste.

Peel and cut all the vegetables finely and mix into curds along with the rest of the above ingredients with the exception of shreded beetroot. Serve decorated with beetroot.

Corn Raita

2 tender corn cobs. 2 cup beaten curds. 1 tsp. cumin seeds. 2 green chillies. ½-inch piece ginger. A few sprigs of corriander leaves. ½ tsp. garam masala. 1 tsp. sugar.

Remove the corn from the cobs and boil in salted water along with a little turmeric powder till tender. Remove from fire and drain out the water. Grind chillies and ginger to a paste.

V. W. G.—2

Mix the chilli paste, sugar, garam masala and corn into the curds. Heat 1 tblsp. ghee. and put in the cumin seeds, when they stop popping, put into the curds. Serve decorated with sprigs of corriander leaves.

Pudina Raita

1 small bunch mint leaves. 2 cups beaten curds. 25 grams raisins. 1 tsp. cumin seeds. Salt and chilli powder to taste.

Grind mint, cumin seeds and raisins to a paste. Mix into the curds with salt and chilli powder and serve cold.

Khajur Raita

200 grams beaten curds. 75 grams dates. $\frac{1}{4}$ coconut. Salt to taste.

Grind dates and coconut to a very fine paste. Mix into curds along with salt and eat with bajri ki roti.

Dhokli Raita

250 grams beaten curds. 50 grams gram flour. 1 tsp. roasted and ground cumin seeds. 1-inch piece ginger, minced. 1 tsp. poppy seeds. 1 tblsp. sugar. 2 green chillies, minced. Handful of sliced corriander leaves. $\frac{1}{2}$ tsp. garam masala. Salt and chilli powder to taste.

Mix flour with salt, ginger, cumin seeds, poppy seeds, chillies, salt and corriander leaves. Mix in enough water to form a thin batter. Put over slow fire and cook till the mixture turns thick and leaves the sides of the vessel. Put in a greased thali and level the surface. Set aside to turn cold and then cut into small pieces. Mix sugar with curds and dhokli pieces. Sprinkle on top garam masala, chilli powder and corriander leaves.

RICE

Masala pullao

250 grams Delhi rice. 250 grams shelled peas. 4 cloves. 2 bay leaves. 1-inch piece cinnamon stick. A big pinch asafoetida. $\frac{1}{4}$ tsp. each of mustard and cumin seeds. 1 small bunch corriander leaves. 4 green chillies slitted. $\frac{1}{2}$ tsp. turmeric powder. 2 big tomatoes, blanched and sliced. 2 tblsps. grated coconut. Salt to taste.

Wash and soak the rice in 500 grams water for 2 hours. Heat 4 tblsps. ghee and add asafoetida, mustard and cumin seeds. When the seeds stop popping add the turmeric and whole spices, salt and tomatoes and cook till the tomatoes turn soft. Add the peas, mix well and then add the rice along with the water in which it was soaked. Bring the water to a boil, reduce heat and cook till the rice is almost done. Put in $\frac{1}{4}$ bunch of the corriander leaves and green chillies after frying them lightly. Continue cooking till the rice is done. Serve decorated with remaining corriander leaves and coconut.

Sweet pullao

250 grams rice. 150 grams sugar. 1 tsp. coarsely pounded cardamom seeds. $\frac{1}{4}$ tsp. finely grated nutmeg. $\frac{1}{2}$ tsp. essence of kewda or rose. 25 grams fried and sliced cashewnuts and raisins and peanuts. 2 tblsps. fried charoli. Silver foil.

Wash and soak rice in water for 2 hours. Drain out the water and dry for 1 hour, then grind it coarsely. Heat 4 tblsps. ghee and fry the rice to light golden colour. Remove from fire. In a large vessel put 2 tblsps. sugar and melt till golden.

Pour in 500 grams water and bring to a boil. Now put in the rice, cardamoms and nutmeg and cook till the rice is tender and dry. Mix in nuts and essence and remove from fire. Cover with foil before serving.

Biraj

2 cups rice. 1 cup cooked channa dal. 2 cups sugar. 1 tsp. cardamom seeds. A few drops essence of saffron. 12 almonds. 12 pistachios and 12 cashewnuts. 25 grams each of raisins and charroli. Silver foil.

Blanch, fry and slice the nuts and raisins. Wash and soak rice in water for a few hours and drain. Heat 4 tblsps. ghee and put in the rice and cardamoms and fry to a light golden colour. Pour in 4 cups water. Bring to a boil, reduce heat and cook till the rice is almost tender and dry. Put in the dal and sugar, mix thoroughly and continue cooking till the rice turns tender and dry. Remove from fire and mix in the nuts, raisins and essence. Serve decorated with foil.

Khichadi

2 cups rice. 1 cup moong dal. 1 large onion, finely sliced. ½ tsp. turmeric powder. 1 tsp. cardamom seeds. 4 cloves. 1-inch piece cinnamon stick, broken into bits. 1-inch piece ginger, minced. 1 tsp. cumin seeds. Salt to taste. 1 small onion, cut into thin rings.

Wash and soak the dal and rice separately in water for a few hours and then drain out the water. Heat 4 tblsps. ghee and add all the whole spices. When they smell, put in the onion and ginger and fry to a light golden colour, add the dal and fry for 5minutes, put in the rice, turmeric and salt and fry again for 5 minutes. Put in enough water to stand one inch above the level of the rice. Bring to a boil, reduce heat and cook till the rice is done. Remove from fire and set aside. Fry the onion rings till golden, spread over rice and serve hot.

Potato pullao

2 cups Delhi rice. 1 cup moong dal. 100 grams baby potatoes. A pinch sugar. 4 cloves. 1-inch piece cinnamon stick. 1 bay leaf, crumpled. 1 tsp. cardamom seeds. 2 medium onions, sliced finely. 1 small onion, cut into thin rings and fried till crisp and golden. 100grams shelled green peas. 1 tsp. cumin seeds. $\frac{1}{2}$ turmeric powder. 1 small piece coconut. 1 small bunch corriander leaves. 4 green chillies. 1-inch piece ginger. 4 flakes garlic. Salt to taste.

Boil potatoes and peal. Also boil peas. Grind coconut, ginger, garlic, chillies and corriander leaves to a paste. Mix in sugar, salt, turmeric and 2 tblsps. curds. Heat 2 tblsps. ghee and fry the potatoes and peas nicely. Mix in the curd mixture and cook till dry.Remove from fire and set aside. Wash and soak the dal and rice for a few hours and drain. Heat 4 tblsp. ghee and put in the whole spices, when they smell, add the onions and fry to light golden colour. Put in 1 tsp. turmeric powder and fry briefly Add rice and dal and fry for 5 minutes. Pour in enough water to stand 1-inch above the level of the rice and bring to a boil. Reduce heat and cook till the rice is almost tender and dry. Take a greased dish and arrange rice and vegetables in layers in it. Start and finish with a layer of rice. Cover tightly and cook over a very low heat till the rice turns tender and completely dry. Serve garnished with fried onions, corriander leaves and if you like fine strips of tomatoes.

Vegetable pullao

450 grams rice. 2 cups coconut milk. 115 grams moong dal. 1 small bunch corriander leaves. 1-inch piece ginger. 4 red and 4 green chillies. 4 flakes garlic. 1 tsp. garam masala. 115 grams onions, cut into thin rings and fried to a golden colour. 1 tblsp. garam masala, $\frac{1}{4}$ tsp. essence of saffron. Juice of half a lime. 450 grams mixed vegetables like cauliflower, carrots, peas, potatoes and french beans. Salt to taste. 250 grams fried cashewnuts. 1 small piece coconut.

Cut cauliflower into flowerets. Cube potatoes, cut carrots into sticks. Shell peas and shred the french beans. Wash and soak the rice and dal for 1 hour in water, drain and half boil both of them separately. Drain out the water and set aside Grind ginger, chillies, corriander leaves and garlic to a paste. Heat 3 tblsps. ghee and fry all the vegetables for 5 minutes. Put in the ground paste, garam masala, turmeric powder and salt. Cover tightly and cook till the vegetables are half cook-ed. Blend coconut milk with lime juice and saffron. Fry the coconut to a golden colour and slice finely. Take a large greased vessel and arrange rice, dal, onions and vegetables in layers in it. Start and finish with a layer of rice. Pour coconut milk on top. Cover tightly, place a heavy weight on the lid and cook over a very slow fire till the rice is tender and dry. You can also cook this in a slow oven. Serve decorated with cashewnuts fried coconut, strips of raw tomato and corriander leaves.

Dal pullao

250 grams rice. 250 grams baby potatoes. 125 grams masoor dal. 100 grams onions, finely sliced 1-inch piece ginger. 5 flakes garlic. ½ tsp. turmeric powder. ½ tsp. sugar. 1 tsp. cumin seeds. 4 cloves. 1-inch piece cinnamon stick, broken into bits. 1 bay leaf, crumpled. Salt to taste. A few sprigs corriander leaves. 1 tiny onion, cut into thin rings and fried to a golden colour. Salt to taste.

Wash and soak rice and dal separately for 1 hour and drain out the water. Peel the potatoes. Grind ginger and garlic to a paste and mix in ½ cup hot water. Heat 4 tblsps. ghee and fry onions to almond colour. Put in whole spices with the exception of cumin seeds and turmeric powder. Fry briefly, then add potatoes and salt and fry for 5 minutes. Put in sugar and garlic water and cook till potatoes are half done. Mix in the rice and dal, then pour in enough water to stand 1-inch above the level of the rice. Bring the water to a boil, reduce heat to simmering and cook till the rice is tender and dry. Put in a serving dish.

Heat 1 tblsp. ghee and toss in the cumin seeds. When they stop popping put over the rice. Garnish with onion rings and sprigs of corriander leaves before serving.

Onion pullao

2 cups boiled rice. 2 big onions, cut into thin rings. $\frac{1}{2}$ tsp. turmeric powder. 1-inch piece ginger, minced. 4 green chillies, minced. $\frac{1}{2}$ tsp. sugar. A few curry leaves. 50 grams fried cashewnuts. Juice of 1 lime. 25 grams fried cashewnuts. Salt to taste. A pinch of asafoetida. $\frac{1}{2}$ tsp. mustard seeds.

Heat 4 tblsps. ghee and add asafoetida and mustard. When the seeds stop popping, add turmeric, fry briefly, then add onions, ginger, curry leaves and chillies. Cook till the onions starts changing colour. Put in the rice, salt and lime juice and sugar. Mix well and remove from fire. Serve decorated with cashewnuts and raisins.

Coconut biraj

250 grams Delhi rice. 2 coconuts, finely grated. A few drops yellow food colouring. $\frac{1}{2}$ tsp. either essence of rose or saffron. 400 grams sugar. 1 tsp. cardamom seeds. 25 grams each of almonds, pistachios, cashewnuts and raisins. Silver foil. 1 tblsp. charoli.

Fry all nuts and raisins in ghee and slice. Fry the grated coconut in ghee to a nice red colour and remove from fire. Wash and soak the rice in water for 1 hour, drain out the water and dry for 1 hour. Heat 3 tblsps. ghee and fry the rice to a

light golden colour. Add coconut and cardamoms and enough water to stand 1-inch above
the level of the rice bring the water to a boil, re ·
duce heat and cover and cook till the rice is almost done. Mix in sugar, nuts and colour and
continue cooking till the rice is tender and dry.
Remove from fire, sprinkle essence on top, cover
with foil and serve hot.

Badshahi pullao

2 cups Delhi rice. 500 grams of mixed vegetables
like potatoes, carrots, french beans, cauliflower,
peas and cucumber. 2 big tomatoes, blanched ar l
sliced. 1 tsp. turmeric powder. 2 bay leaves. 2
cardamoms. 4 cloves. 6 peppercorns. ½-inch piece
cinnamon stick, broken into bits. 1 tsp. black or
shahjeera. 25 grams each of almonds, pistachios,
cashewnuts and raisins. 1 tsp. essence of rose or
saffron. 1 tsp. sugar. 2 medium onions, sliced
finely. 1-inch piece ginger, minced. 1 tblsp. til. A
pinch asafoetida. 4 green chillies, slitted. A handful of corriander leaves. Few curry leaves. Salt
to taste. 2 tblsps. grated coconut.

Wash and soak rice in water for 1 hour. Drain
out the water and dry for 1 hour. Fry all the nuts
and raisins and slice them finely. Heat 4 tblsps.
ghee and add asafoetida and all the whole spices
with the exception of shahjeera. When the spices
start smelling, add ginger and onions and fry till
soft. Put in tomatoes, salt and sugar and turmeric powder and coconut and cook till the tomatoes turn soft. Peel and slice the vegetables and
put in. Fry for 5 minutes, then cover tightly and

cook without adding water till the vegetables are almost done, mix in rice, curry and corriander leaves. Then pour in enough water to stand 1-inch above the level of the rice. Bring the water to a boil, reduce heat to simmering and cook till the rice is almost done. Fry chillies lightly and mix in. Continue cooking till the rice is tender and completely dry. Remove from fire and put in a serving dish. Sprinkle nuts, raisins and essence and shahjeera and til on top, then pour 3 tblsps. smoking ghee on whole and serve immediately.

Dahi-dudh nu pullao

2 cups Delhi rice. 250 grams curds. 1 cup milk. 1 tblsp. sugar. 400 grams mixed vegetables like baby potatoes, peas, french beans, carrots and cauliflower. 1 bay leaf, crumpled. 8 peppercorns. 4 cloves. 2 cardamoms. 1-inch piece cinnamon stick, broken into bits. 1 tsp. essence of saffron. 25 grams each of cashewnuts, raisins and charoli. 1 big onion, cut into thin rings. Silver or golden foil. A few drops each of red, green and orange food colouring.

Peel and slice vegetables and half boil them. Wash the rice and half boil in water and then drain out the water. Fry all the nuts and raisins. Also fry onion to a golden colour. Drain and mix with nuts. Divide the rice into 4 portions. Colour one portion red, the second green, the third orange and leave one portion white. Heat 3 tblsps. ghee and toss in all the whole spices, when they smell, put in the vegetables and salt, mix well and remove from fire. Take a big greased dekchi and put in a layer of red rice, cover with a layer of curds, on this put a layer of vegetables, sprinkle nuts and onions on top and then little sugar. On this put a layer of green rice and repeat the process till all the ingredients have been used up and the uppermost layer is a layer of orange rice. Pour on top milk and essence. Cover the dekchi with airtight lid and seal the edges with dough, and cook over a slow fire for ½ hour. Remove from fire and cover with foil before serving.

SWEETS & DESSERTS

Mohanthal

500 grams gram flour. 500 grams ghee. $\frac{1}{2}$ cup milk. 250 grams unsweetened mava or khoya. 350 grams sugar. 2 tblsps. coarsely pounded cardamom seeds. $\frac{1}{2}$ tsp. essence of saffron. 25 grams each of charoli, almonds and pistachio nuts. Silver foil.

Add 50 grams of ghee to flour and mix nicely. Put in the milk, mix thoroughly and pass through a fine sieve. Put 2 cups water in sugar and prepare a syrup of one-thread consistency. Remove from fire and keep it warm. Blanch and slice all the nuts. Heat the remaining ghee and fry the flour till it turns golden coloured and a nice smell emanates from it. Add khoya, cardamoms and nuts and cook till the mixture turns smooth and khoya turns a nice brown colour. Add syrup and keep on stirring till the mixture turns thick and leaves the sides of the vessel add essence. Put the mixture in a greased thali, level the surface, cover with foil and set aside to turn cold, then cut into small pieces and store in airtight container.

Kaju pak

$\frac{1}{2}$ kilo unsweetened khoya. $\frac{3}{4}$ kilo cashewnuts. 500 grams sugar. 1 tsp. either essence of rose or kewda. 1 tsp. coarsely pounded cardamom seeds. 25 grams each of blanched and sliced almonds and pistachios. Silver foil.

Pound the cashewnuts to a powder. Put 2 cups of water in sugar and prepare a syrup of one-thread consistency. Mix in the khoya and stir till the mixture turns smooth. Put in cashewnuts along with all the nuts and cardamoms and keep on stirring till the mixture turns thick and leaves the sides of the vessel. Mix in the essence and remove from fire. Put the mixture in a greased thali, level the surface and cover with foil. Set aside to turn cold then cut into any shape you like. Store in airtight container.

Copra Pak

1 big coconut, finely grated. 1 litre milk. 250 grams sugar. A few drops of orange red colour. 25 grams sliced pistachio nuts. 1 tsp. cardamom seeds. 1 tsp. either essence of rose or kewda.

Place the milk in a heavy-bottomed vessel and cook over a slow fire till it turns and leaves the sides of the vessel. Remove from fire and set aside. Put 2 cups water in sugar and prepare a syrup of one-thread consistency. Put in the thick milk and mix till smooth. Add coconut and cardamom seeds and keep on stirring till the mixture turns thick and leaves the sides of the vessel. Remove from fire and mix in the essence. Put half of the mixture in a greased thali. Colour the remaining mixture a light orange red colour and put on top. Level the surface, sprinkle pistachios on top. Cool thoroughly and cut in any shape you like. Store in airtight tins.

Badam pak

125 grams almonds. 250 grams unsweetened mava or khoya. 125 grams sugar. 1 tsp. carda-

mom seeds. $\frac{1}{2}$ tsp. essence of rose. 75 grams hot ghee. Silver foil.

Blanch the almonds, toast and grind them to a fine powder. Take a heavy-bottomed vessel and put in 2 tblsps. sugar. Mix nicely till the sugar turns pale golden colour. Now add the remaining sugar and add enough water to just cover the sugar. When the sugar melts and forms a thick syrup, add khoya and mix till smooth. Put in almonds and cardamoms and cook till the mixture turns thick. Put in a little ghee at a time. When all the ghee is used up and it starts leaving the pak. Mix in the essence and remove from fire. Put the mixture in a greased thali, level the surface and cover with foil. Let it cool thoroughly then cut into any shapes you like. Store in air tight tin.

Corn pak

4 large tender corn cobs. 6 tblsps. melted ghee. 2 litres milk, 1 tblsp. cardamom seeds. 2 tblsps. poppy seeds. 25 grams each of almonds and pistachios. $1\frac{1}{4}$ tea cups sugar. A few drops either essence of rose or kewda. Silver foil.

Place milk on a slow fire and cook stirring often until the milk turns thick and leaves the sides of the dekchi. Grate corn on a fine grater. Heat ghee and fry the grated corn stirring all the time until it turns light golden coloured. Remove and set aside. Blanch and slice the nuts. Put $\frac{1}{2}$ cup water in sugar and prepare a syrup of one-thread consistency. Add the thick milk and mix it well into the syrup. Add the nuts, corn, cardamoms and poppy seeds. Keep on stirring till the mixture turns thick and leaves the sides of the dekchi. Stir in essence and remove from fire. Put the mixture in a greased thali and level the surface. Cover with foil and set aside to cool thoroughly Cut into pieces and store in airtight tin.

Gaunder pak

500 grams urad dal flour. 125 grams eating gaund. 500 grams sugar. 10 grams each of dry ginger powder, ground peppercorns, cardamoms and nutmeg. 25 grams each of cashewnuts, almonds, pistachios and charoli. Silver foil. 500 grams ghee.

Heat ghee and put in the gaund. When it puffs, drain and pound to a powder. In the same ghee put in the flour and fry it to a nice golden colour. Remove and set aside. Put 2 cups water in sugar and prepare a syrup of one-thread consistency. Put in the flour with the rest of the above ingredients and keep on stirring till the mixture turns thick and leaves the sides of the vessel. Put in a greased thali and level the surface. Cover with foil and cut into any shape you like when cold. This pak is made and eaten in the cold season only.

Poha pak

500 grams fine poha. 125 grams ghee. 500 grams sugar. 1 tsp. cardamom powder. A big pinch of grated jaiphal. 25 grams each of sliced raisins, cashewnuts and charoli. Silver foil.

Wash the poha nicely in water and squeeze out all the moisture. Put 2 cups water in sugar and prepare a syrup of one-thread consistency. Remove from fire and keep it warm. Heat ghee put in poha and fry it to a golden colour. Add the syrup and the nuts with the rest of the ingredients and keep on stirring till the mixture turns thick and leaves the sides of the vessel. Put in a greased thali. Level the surface and cover with foil. Cool thoroughly and cut into any shape you like. Store in airtight container.

Kola pak

1 kilo Red bhopla. 500 grams sugar. 500 grams khoya or mava. 25 grams each of blanched and sliced almonds, pistachios and charoli 25 grams melon seeds. Silver foil. A few drops each of orange red colour and essence of saffron.

Peel and grate the bhopla finely. Then cook over a slow fire without adding water till it turns completely tender and dry. Put in the sugar and keep on stirring till the mixture turns dry again. Add khoya and nuts and mix till the mixture turns thick and leaves the sides of the vessel. Add colour and essence and remove from fire. Put in a greased thali, level the surface and cover with foil. Cool thoroughly and cut into any shape you like. Store in airtight container.

Sukri

500 grams each of ghee, flour and finely grated jaggery. $\frac{1}{4}$ dry coconut, sliced finely. 1 tblsp. each

of cardamoms and poppy seeds. 25 grams each of sliced almonds and pistachios and charoli. A few halved almonds.

Roast the flour to a brown colour in a dry pan over a slow fire. Heat ghee, add jaggery and stir till the jaggery dissolves. Put in the flour and the rest of the above ingredients with the exception of halved almonds and cook till the mixture turns thick and leaves the sides of the vessel. Put in a greased thali, level the surface and decorate with almonds. Set aside to cool thoroughly and then cut into any shape you like. Store in airtight container.

Gol papadi

½ coconut, finely grated. 1 cup ghee. 2 cups each of flour and finely grated jaggery. 1 tsp. cardamom seeds. A pinch of grated nutmeg. A few sliced almonds and pistachios.

Heat ghee and fry the flour to a nice golden colour. Put in the rest of the above ingredients with the exception of nuts and keep on stirring till the mixture turns thick and leaves the sides of the vessel. Put in a greased thali, level the surface and decorate with sliced nuts. Set aside to turn cold then cut into any shape you like.

Dudhpak

½ litre milk. 2 tblsps. rice. ¼ cup sugar. A few drops each of orange red colour and essence of saffron. 25 grams each of blanched and sliced almonds, pistachios, charoli and melon seeds. Silver foil.

Soak the rice in water for a few hours and then drain out the water. Now put the rice in milk and keep on slow fire. Cook till the rice turns tender and mixture quite thick. Remove from fire, stir in nuts, essence and colour. Serve either hot or cold covered with foil.

Chickoo ka dudhpak

½ litre milk. 6 ripe chickoos. 4 tblsps. sugar. ½ tsp. essence of rose. 25 grams each of sliced almonds, pistachios, charoli and melon seeds.

Put milk on slow fire and cook till the mixture turns thick. Then keep on stirring till it turns light golden in colour. Add sugar and keep stirring till it dissolves and the mixture turns thick. Remove from fire and add essence and chill. Peel the chickoos, remove seeds and mash to a paste. Put into the chilled milk and serve decorated with nuts.

Basundi

½ litre milk. 25 grams each of almonds, pistachio nuts, charoli, raisins and melon seeds. A few drops each of orange red colour and essence of either saffron or rose. Silver foil. 4 tblsps. sugar. Place milk over a slow fire and cook till the milk is reduced to three-fourths of the original quantity. Put in finely sliced nuts and 1 tsp. cardamom seeds and remove from fire. Add colour and essence and serve it chilled covered with foil.

Puran poli

250 grams maida. Salt to taste

For filling......125 grams channa dal. 1 cup finely grated jaggery. 1 tsp. coarsely powdered cardamom seeds. 25 grams each of sliced almonds, pistachios, charoli and raisins.

Mix together flour and salt, rub in 2 tblsps. ghee and then put enough water to form a stiff dough. Soak the dal in water for a few hours. Drain and cook with little water until soft and completely dry. Remove from fire and grind to a coarse paste and then mix with all the filling ingredients. Divide the dough and the filling into equal number of portions. Shape each portion into a ball and roll out each ball into a round puri or disc. Spread the mixture nicely and evenly over one round and cover with the other round. Seal and pinch the edges nicely together and roll out into a little bigger puri with the help of a little dry flour. Shallow fry to a golden brown colour. Serve either hot or cold.

Khoya poli

200 grams maida. 2 tblsps. sugar. $\frac{1}{2}$ cup milk. 2 tsps. ghee.

For filling...... 50 grams sweetened khoya. 2 tblsps. grated coconut. 25 grams each of sliced charoli and raisins. A few sliced almonds and pistachios. $\frac{1}{2}$ tsp. cardamom powder. A few drops essence of rose.

Mix together all the filling ingredients. Dissolve sugar in milk. Rub ghee into flour and then add enough milk to form a stiff dough. Divide the dough and the filling into equal number of portions and then form polis as shown in the above recipe.

Flour Sheera

3 tblsps. flour. 2 cups milk. 1 tsp. coarsely pounded cardamom seeds. 1 tblsp. charoli. A few sliced almonds and pistachios. 3 tblsps. sugar.

Dissolve sugar in milk. Heat 2 tblsps. ghee and fry the flour to a red colour. Add milk and cardamoms and cook till the mixture turns thick. Serve hot decorated with nuts.

Corn Sheera

4 tender corn cobs. 2 cups milk. A few drops essence of saffron. A few sliced almonds and pistachios. 1 tblsp. charoli. ½ tsp. cardamom powder. 4 tblsps. sugar.

Grate the corn over a fine grater. Heat 4 tblsps. ghee and fry the corn stirring all the time till it turns light golden. Put in milk and cardamoms and cook till the milk is absorbed, add sugar and stir continuously till the sugar melts and the mixture is thick. Remove from fire and sprinkle essence on top. Serve either hot or cold decorated with nuts.

Dal Sheera

1 cup moong dal. 1 cup sugar. 2 cup milk ¼ cup ghee. 2 cloves, 25 grams each of chopped raisins and cashewnuts. 1 tblsp. charoli. ½ tsp. cardamom powder. A few drops either essence of rose or saffron.

Soak dal in water for a few hours. Drain out the water and grind coarsely. Heat ghee and cloves, when they smell, add dal and fry to a nice red colour. Put in the milk and cardamom powder and cook over a slow fire till the mixture turns dry. Add sugar and continue cooking till the sheera turns dry once again. Remove from fire and put in essence, serve hot or cold decorated with nuts.

Magaz

500 grams gram flour. 250 grams sugar. 250 grams ghee. 50 grams khoya. 25 grams each of blanched and sliced almonds, pistachios and charoli. 1 tblsp. cardamom seeds. Silver foil.

Put 2 cups water in sugar and prepare a syrup of one-thread consistancy. Remove from fire and keep it warm. Heat ghee add flour and fry to a red colour. Put in the khoya and cardamoms, mix till smooth. Put in the nuts and syrup and cook till the mixture turns thick and leaves the sides of the vessel. Put in a greased thali, level the surface and cover with foil. Set aside to turn cold and then cut into any shape you like. Store in airtight tin.

Malpura

1 cup maida. 1 tblsp. rava. 4 tblsps. sugar. A few drops essence of saffron. A pinch of baking powder. 1 tblsp. each of sliced raisins and charoli. A few sliced almonds and pistachios.

Mix together all the above ingredients with the exception of sugar. Dissolve sugar in ½ cup water and mix into the flour mixture to form a batter. The mixture should be a thick batter If you do not have the right consistency of batter add a little flour or water to make the right consistency. Heat enough ghee for deep frying to smoking, lower the heat, then put in 1 tblsp. of batter. Spread the batter into a thin round shape and fry over a slow fire to a nice golden colour. Drain nicely and serve hot.

Lapsi

250 grams wheat. 250 grams finely grated jaggery. 1 tsp. cardamom seeds. 1 tblsp. anise seeds. 25 grams black raisins. 25 grams fried groundnuts.

Coarsely pound the wheat. Dissolve jaggery in 2 glasses of water. Strain and keep aside. Heat 6 tblsps. ghee and fry the wheat to a golden colour. Put in jaggery water anise seeds and cardamoms. Bring to a boil, reduce heat to simmering and cook stirring occasionally till the wheat is tender and completely dry. When done the grains should be separate and not mushy or sticking together. Serve decorated with raisins and peanuts.

Chickoo Pak

12 good quality ripe and sweet chickoos. 1 cup sugar. 125 grams khoya. A few drops essence of rose. A few sliced cashewnuts and charoli. A big pinch grated nutmeg. ½ tsp. powdered cardamoms. A few drops red food colouring. 1 tblsp. ghee. Silver foil.

Peel and mash the chickoos nicely. Heat ghee and fry them till dry. Add khoya and mix till smooth. Put in the nuts, sugar, cardamoms and nutmeg and cook till the mixture turns thick and starts leaving the sides of the vessel. Put in essence and enough red colour to give the pak a nice pink colour. Put in a greased thali, level the surface, cover with foil and cool before cutting into pieces.

Dahi Pak

1 litre milk. 1 kilo curds. 400 grams sugar. 100 grams each of almonds and pistachios. 2 tblsps. charoli. 1 tsp. cardamom powder. $\frac{1}{2}$ tsp. essence of saffron. Silver foil.

Pour the curds in a clean muslin cloth and tie loosely. Hang the bag for 2 to 3 hours to enable all the liquid to drip through. Put milk on a slow fire and keep stirring occassionally till the milk turns thick. Remove from fire. Blanch and slice all the nuts finely. Tie a strong cloth over a pan. Take small quantity of sugar, thick milk and curds and mix well over the cloth and put in a clean bowl. Continue doing this till all the mixture is used up. Now mix in the rest of the above ingredients with the exception of foil and put in a greased thali. Steam till firm. Remove from heat, cover with foil, cool and cut into pieces.

Kansar

1 cup coarse rava-like wheat flour. 1 tblsp. seeds of large black cardamoms ½ cup grated jaggery.

25 grams roasted and pounded groundnuts. 25 grams fried and sliced raisins.

Rub 2 tblsps. ghee into the flour and pass through a fine sieve. Heat 2 cups water and bring it to a boil, reduce heat and add jaggery. When the jaggery dissolves, put in the raisins, nuts and flour and cook stirring often till the mixture turns thick and leaves the sides of the vessel. Remove from fire, cool till bearably hot and form into small round and flat balls. Press a few grains of cardamoms on both sides and serve with pure ghee.

Gheun ka Dudhpak

1 litre milk, 125 grams sugar. 50 grams cracked wheat. 1 tsp. cardamom seeds, powdered.

Wash the wheat and soak in water for 1 hour. Drain out the water and remove outer peel or skin by rubbing with a cloth. Bring milk to a boil. Put in the wheat and cook till the wheat is tender and the milk thick. Add the sugar and keep on stirring till the pak turns almond coloured. Serve sprinkled with cardamom powder.

Shrikhand

500 grams curds. 150 grams sugar. 1 tsp. cardamom powder. 25 grams each of sliced cashewnuts, blanched and sliced almonds and pistachios. 1 tblsp. charoli. ½ tsp. essence of saffron.

Powder a few pistachios and mix with cardamom powder and charoli and set aside. Put curds into a clean muslin cloth and tie loosely. Hang the bag for 2 to 3 hours to enable all the water to drip through. Tie a strong cloth on a dekchi and take small quantity of curds and sugar and mix well over the cloth. Put into a clean bowl. When all the curds and sugar are used up, add saffron and sliced nuts. Springle on top cardamom mixture. Chill and serve with piping hot plain puries.

PURIES, THEPLAS & ROTLIES

Methi Puri

250 grams flour. 1 bunch fenugreek leaves. 4 green chillies, minced. 1 small tomato, peeled and sliced. Salt to taste.

Clean and slice the leaves.. Sprinkle salt on top and set aside for 15 minutes, then squeeze out all the moisture and wash in 3 to 4 changes of water, drain and put in a pan along with the rest of the above ingredients with the exception of flour. Cover tightly and cook till the methi is tender. Remove from fire, cool and add flour, add enough water to form a stiff dough. Divide the dough into small balls and roll each ball into a round puri or disc. Deap fry each puri to a golden brown colour. Drain and serve piping hot.

Jeera Puri

125 grams each of maida and flour. 1 tsp. each of coarsely pounded cumin seeds and peppercorns. Salt to taste.

Blend together all the above ingredients. Rub in 2 tblsps. ghee, then add enough water to form a stiff dough. Divide the dough into small balls and roll out each ball into a round puri. Make holes into each puri with a needle and deep fry till crisp and golden. Serve hot or cool nicely and store in airtight container.

Masala puri

250 grams flour. A pinch asafoetida. ½ tsp. turmeric powder. 1 tblsp. til. 1 tsp. ground cumin seeds. Salt to taste.

Mix together all the above ingredients. Rub in 2 tblsps. ghee and then add enough water to form a stiff dough. Divide the dough into small balls and roll out each ball into a round puri. Make holes in each puri with the help of a needle and deep fry till crisp and golden. Drain and serve immediately or store in airtight container.

Mithi puri

250 grams maida. 50 grams sugar. Milk. 1 tsp. powdered cardamom seeds. A few drops essence of saffron. A pinch nutmeg.

Cover sugar with milk and set aside till the sugar dissolves into the Mix together the remaining ingredients. Rub in 2 tblsps. ghee and then add enough milk to form a stiff dough. Divide the dough into small balls and roll out each ball into a puri. Make holes into the puri with a needle and deep fry till crisp and golden. Drain, serve hot or cool nicely and store in airtight tin.

Dahi puri

2 cups flour. 1 cup maida. 1 tsp. each of coarsely pounded peppercorns, cumin seeds and turmeric powder. Beaten curds. Salt to taste.

Blend together all the above ingredients with the exception of curds. Rub in 1 tblsp. ghee and then add enough curds to form a stiff dough. Form the dough into puris and deep fry to a golden brown colour. Drain and serve piping hot.

Vegetable puri

2 cups flour. 1 big potato. 1 carrot. A few cabbage leaves. A couple of french beans. 4 green
chillies, minced. 1 small bunch finely sliced corriander leaves. 1 tsp. ground cumin seeds. $\frac{1}{4}$ tsp.
garam masala. $\frac{1}{2}$ tsp. turmeric powder. Salt to
taste.

Peel and steam all the vegetables then mash to a
paste. Blend together flour and all the spices.
Rub in 2 tblsps. ghee then add all the vegetables
with all the remaining ingredients. Mix well then
put in enough water to form a stiff dough. Divide
the dough into small balls. Roll the balls into
puris and deep fry to a golden colour. Drain and
serve hot.

Potato puri

250 grams flour. 250 grams boiled, peeled and
mashed potatoes. $\frac{1}{2}$ tsp. each of cumin seeds,
garam masala and turmeric powder. 1 small
bunch finely sliced corriander leaves. 3 green
chillies, minced. 1 tblsp. melted ghee. Salt to taste.

Mix together all the above ingredients and add
very little water to form a stiff dough. Form the
dough into puris and deep fry to a golden brown
colour. Serve piping hot.

Bhakri

450 grams flour. 115 grams nicely beaten sour
curds. $\frac{1}{2}$ tsp. turmeric powder. Pinch of asafoetida. 55 grams melted ghee. Salt and pepper to
taste.

Mix together all the dry ingredients. Rub in ghee, then add curds and form a smooth dough. Set aside for 1 hour. Divide the dough into balls. Roll out each ball into a round chapati and shallow fry to a golden brown colour. Serve hot.

Puffed chapati

250 grams flour. Salt to taste.

Rub ghee into the flour then add enough water to form quite a stiff dough. Divide the dough into lime-sized balls and roll out each ball into a small puri. Now take one puri and apply a little ghee on it place another puri, sprinkle flour on top and roll out into a round chapati. Place the chapati on a hot girdle. After a minute, turn over the chapati and press all over with a cloth till the chapati is baked and puffed. Remove from fire and smear liberally with ghee. Serve with Aamb Rus. Take 6 sweet mangoes and roast them over a dry girdle till they turn soft. Squeeze out the pulp and strain through a cloth. In each glass of rus put in ¼ tsp. dry ginger powder, 1 tsp. ground cumin seeds, salt to taste and 1 tblsp. melted ghee.

Thepla of Methi

500 grams flour. Pinch of asafoetida. 1 tsp. turmeric powder. 25 grams each of bajra and gram flour. 4 green chillies. 1 bunch fenugreek leaves cleaned and sliced. A pinch soda. 2 tblsps. oil. Salt and chilli powder to suit the taste.

Mix together all the above ingredients then add enough water to form quite a stiff dough. Divide into balls and roll out each ball into a round chapati. Shallow fry to a golden brown colour. Serve hot with raita of your choice.

Mulana thepla

500 grams wheat flour. 3 radishes, peeled and grated. 4 green chillies, minced. A handful of sliced corriander leaves. Pinch asafoetida. 1 tsp turmeric powder. Salt to taste. 2 tblsps. oil.

Mix together all the above ingredients with the exception of radishes. Squeeze out water from radishes and add, then add enough water to form quite a stiff dough. Then prepare and fry like above thepla.

Dal nu thepla

2 cups toovar dal. 1¼ cup flour. 1 tsp. dhania jeera. 1 tsp. turmeric powder. Handful of sliced corriander leaves. 4 green chillies, minced. 1-inch piece ginger, minced. Salt to taste.

Wash and soak dal in water for 1 hour, then boil in the water in which it was soaked till it turns very soft. Mash to a paste and mix in the rest of the above ingredients and cook till the mixture turns thick. Remove from fire, cool and knead to a smooth dough. Divide into small balls and roll out each ball into a round chapati and shallow fry to a golden brown colour. Drain and serve piping hot.

Moong and potato Rotla

2 cups flour. 2 medium potatoes. ½ cup moong dal. 4 green chillies, minced. 1-inch piece ginger,

minced. Handful of sliced corriander leaves.
Salt, chilli powder and lime juice to taste.

Boil the dal till soft and dry. Boil, peel and
mash the potatoes and mix with all the above ingredients with the exception of flour. Put salt
into flour along with enough water to from a stiff
dough. Divide the dough into small balls. Now
roll out 2 balls of dough into small puries. Cover
one puri evenly with a tablespoon of filling and
cover it with the other puri, seal and pinch the
edges together, sprinkle a little dry flour on top
and roll out carefully and gently into a bigger
round. Shallow fry to a golden brown colour
and serve piping hot after liberally applying ghee
or butter to it.

Batata nu rotla

2 cups flour. 2 big potatoes, boiled, peeled and
mashed. 1 tsp. each of dhania jeera and sugar. $\frac{1}{4}$
tsp. garam masala. 2 tblsps. finely grated coconut.
Handful of sliced corriander leaves. Salt, lime
juice and chilli powder to suit the taste.

Put salt and enough water in flour to form a stiff
dough. Mix the rest of the ingredients together.
Now make and fry the rotlas in the same way as
shown in the above recipe.

Dal nu rotla

2 cups flour. 1$\frac{1}{2}$ cups whole moong. 2 tblsps.
grated coconut. $\frac{1}{2}$ tsp. each of dhania jeera and
garam masala. Handful of sliced corriander
leaves. 3 green chillies, minced. Salt, chilli powder and lime juice to taste.

Wash and soak dal in water whole night. Next morning, drain out the water and tie in a cloth and hang from a nail in the wall for 24 hours at the end of which you will see that the dal has developed sprouts. Boil the dal in water till soft and dry, then mix in the rest of the above ingredients and remove from fire. Mix flour with salt and then add enough water to form a stiff dough. Now prepare and fry the rotlas in the same way as shown in the recipe entitled "Moong and potato rotla".

Vegetable Rotla

2 cups flour. 50 grams each of peas, carrots and pumpkin. 1-inch piece ginger, minced. 4 green chillies, minced. 2 tblsps. grated coconut. Handful of sliced corriander leaves. ½ tsp. each of garam masala and dhania jeera. Salt, lime juice and chilli powder to taste.

Put salt and enough water in flour to form a stiff dough. Peel and steam the vegetables. Mash nicely and mix with the remaining ingredients. Now prepare and fry the rotlas in the same way as shown in the receipe entitled "moong and potato rotla".

Batatanu bhakri

2 cups wheat flour. 3 medium potatoes, boiled peeled and mashed. 1 tblsp. gram flour. 1-inch piece ginger, minced. 3 green chillies, minced Handful of sliced corria nder leaves. A few curry leaves. Pinch of asafoetiaa ½ tsp. each of turmeric powder and mu to seeds. 1 cup sou

curds. 2 to 3 tblsps. grated jaggery. Salt and chilli powder to taste.

Heat 1 tblsp. oil and add asafoetida and mustard. When the seeds stop popping, put in gram flour and fry to a red colour. Now put in all the above ingredients with the exception of flour, potatoes and jaggery. Cook over a slow fire till the curds turn dry. Remove from fire and mix in potatoes and jaggery. Put salt and enough water in flour to form a' stiff dough. Now prepare and fry the bhakri in the sameway as shown in the recipe entitled "moong and potato rotla."

Bajra rotli

2 cups bajra flour. Salt to taste.

Mix together flour and salt and then add enough water to form a stiff dough. Divide the dough into lime-sized balls and shape each ball into a thick and round rotli on your hand. Place on a well-greased girdle or tava and continue flattening by pressing all round with the palm of the hand, taking care not to break it. Cook on both the sides on slow fire. Serve hot smeared liberally with ghee or butter.

Methi and bajri rotli

2 cups bajra flour. ½ bunch fenugreek leaves, cleaned and sliced. 2 green chillies, minced. Handful of sliced corriander leaves. 1 small piece minced ginger. Salt to taste.

Mix together all the above ingredients with

enough water to form a stiff dough, now prepare
and fry the rotli in the same way as shown in the
above recipe.

PICKLES & CHUTNEYS

Hot mango pickle

1 kilo raw and tender green mangoes. 100 grams fenugreek seeds. 100 grams coarsely pounded fenugreek seeds. 50 grams yellow mustard dal. 1 tsp. asafoetida. 100 grams chilli powder. 100 grams mustard oil. Salt.

Cut mangoes into four halfway through. Soak whole fenugreek seeds in water whole night, next morning drain out the water and set aside to dry for 1 hour. Heat oil and put in whole fenugreek seeds and asafoetida. When the seeds stop popping and turn red, put in the mustard dal and remaining fenugreek seeds, fry briefly and remove from fire. Cool and put in salt, chilli powder and 2 tsps. turmeric powder. Mix well and stuff the masala nicely into each mango. Put the mangoes in a jar with a tight-fitting lid and set aside for 3 days. Then pour in enough mustard oil to stand 1-inch above the level of the mangoes. Set aside for 15 days before eating this pickle. This pickle lasts for a few years.

Spicy mango pickle

30 raw very tender large mangoes. 1 kilo salt. 1 tea cup coarsely ground fenugreek seeds. ½ tblsp. asafoetida. 6 tblsps. turmeric powder. 10 cloves. 4-inch piece cinnamon stick, broken into bits. 1 cup coarsely pounded mustard seeds. 1 cup chilli powder. 1 kilo til oil. ¾ cup castor oil.

Mix turmeric powder in castor oil and set aside. Wash and cut the mangoes into small pieces. Apply castor oil on them and set them aside for 1 hour. Broil the salt on girdle and set aside.

Heat the oil and add asafoetida. When it dissolves, add the rest of the spices and salt. Remove from fire, cool and put in the mangoes. Put in a clean airtight jar and set aside for 2 weeks. This pickle lasts for 1 year.

Mango and vegetable pickle

2½ kilos tender and raw mangoes. 125 grams yellow mustard dal. 50 grams fenugreek seeds. 100 grams chilli powder. 100 grams magaz of corriander seeds. 50 grams anise seeds. 500 grams carrots. 100 grams each of tindlis and cluster beans or gavar. 1½ kilo mustard oil. Salt. Turmeric powder.

Peel and slice the mangoes. Sprinkle on them salt and turmeric powder liberally and set them aside in a covered bottle for 3 days. Squeeze out all the water and set aside. Peel and cube the carrots, string the beans and slit the tindlis halfway through. Peel 50 grams garlic. Pound together fenugreek and anise seeds. Heat ½ kilo oil to smoking and toss in garlic and all the spices with the exception of mustard. Fry nicely and remove from fire. Cool and mix in all the vegetables, mustard and mangoes. Put in a jar with a tight-fitting lid. Now heat the remaining oil to smoking and pour in. Cover tightly and set aside for 2 weeks. This pickle lasts for 1 year.

Chundo No. 1

1 kilo raw mangoes, peeled and grated finely. ½ kilo sugar. 1 tblsp. ground cumin seeds. 2 tblsps. chilli powder. Salt. Turmeric powder.

Mix salt and turmeric into the mangoes and set aside for a few hours, squeeze out all the water and set aside. Put 3 cups water in sugar and prepare a syrup of one-thread consistency. Put in the mangoes and cook over a slow fire till the mangoes turns soft. Mix in the rest of the above spices and remove from fire. Cool and bottle.

Chundo No. 2

1 kilo raw mangoes, finely grated. ¾ kilo sugar. 1 tblsp. cardamom seeds, 25 grams each of blanched and sliced almonds and pistachios.

Place the mangoes and sugar in a airtight bottle. Set in the sun for 15 days, then mix in the rest of the above ingredients. This pickle lasts from 6 months to 1 year.

Red capsicum pickle

2½ kilos red capsicums. 125 grams magaz of corriander seeds. 250 grams yellow mustard dal. 50 grams each of anise and fenugreek seeds. 1 cup strained lime juice. 250 grams salt.

Slit the capsicums into four halfway through. Powder coarsely anise and fenugreek seeds. Mix together lime juice, spices and salt and fill into each capsicum. Put in a airtight bottle and set aside for 5 days.

Lime pickle

25 limes. 25 grams grated jaggery. 100 grams each of fresh green ginger and thick green chillies. 1 tsp. asafoetida. Salt to taste.

Boil limes in water till soft. Drain out the water and cut into small pieces. Also cut chillies and turmeric into pieces. Mix together all the above ingredients and put in a airtight bottle. Eat after 1 week.

Chilli pickle

1 kilo thick and long green chillies. 125 grams each of salt and yellow mustard dal. Strained juice of 4 big limes. 1 tsp. castor oil. 2 tblsps. turmeric powder.

Slit each chilli in the middle halfway through. Stuff with salt and set aside for 2 days. Remove from salt and set aside for a few hours to dry. Pound mustard and mix with the rest of the above ingredients and stuff into each chilli. Put in an airtight bottle and eat after 3 to 4 days.

Amla murraba

1 kilo amla. 2 kilos sugar. $\frac{1}{4}$ tsp. each of pan-ka-chuna and alum. A few drops essence of saffron.

Poke each amla nicely with a sharp needle all over. Dissolve alum and chuna in water and soak the amlas in it for 1 hour. Wash in water and boil them till they are soft. Drain out the water and set aside. Put 4 cups water in sugar and prepare a syrup of one-thread consistency. Put in the amlas and cook over a slow fire till the syrup turns quite thick. Remove from fire, cool, mix in essence and put in airtight bottle. Eat after 4 days.

Amla ka chunda

2½ kilo amlas. 2 tblsps. ghee. 5 kilos sugar. 15 grams each of tejpatte or bay leaves, cloves, dry ginger and cardamoms. A few drops essence of saffron. 2 nutmegs. 2 tblsps. ghee.

Poke each amla nicely with a sharp needle all over. Dissolve a tsp. each of alum and pan-ka-chuna in water and soak the amlas in it for 1 hour. Drain out the water and boil in clean water till soft. Drain and grind to a paste. Pound together all the spices. Fry the paste lightly in ghee and set aside.

Put 2 glasses of water in sugar and prepare a syrup of one-thread consistency. Put in the amla paste and cook till the mixture turns thick. Remove from fire, mix in the rest of the ingredients and cool and bottle. Eat after 1 day.

Gaurkerry

1 kilo raw mangoes, peeled and sliced. 1½ kilos grated jaggery. 250 grams til oil. 2 tblsps. chilli powder. 1 tblsp. salt. 1 tsp. asafoetida.

Heat the oil to smoking and add asofoetida, when it melts, add the mango slices and fry till soft. Put in the salt, jaggery and the remaining ingredients and cook till the mixture turns thick. Remove from fire. Cool and bottle.

Chilli chutney

25 grams roasted groundnuts. 6 green chillies. 1 small bunch corriander leaves. strained juice of

1 lime. Salt to taste. 1 small piece ginger. 1 tsp. sugar.

Grind together sugar, groundnuts, chillies, corriander leaves and ginger to a paste and mix in lime juice and salt.

Gram chutney

100 grams roasted grams or channa. Handful of mint leaves. 1 small bunch of corriander leaves. 1 lime-sized ball of tamarind. 4 green chillies. Salt to taste.

Cover tamarind with 1 cup water for 5 minutes and then squeeze out the juice. Grind together the remaining ingredients and mix into the tamarind pulp.

Corriander chutney

1 bunch corriander leaves. ¼ coconut. 4 flakes garlic. 4 green chillies 1 small ball of tamarind. 1 small piece ginger. 1 tblsp. sugar. A few leaves of mint. 1 small onion. Salt to taste.

Soak tamarind in little water for 5 minutes then squeeze out the pulp. Grind the remaining ingredients to a paste and mix into the tamarind pulp.

Peanut chutney

25 grams roasted peanuts. 3 roasted red chillies. 1 small piece ginger. 1 tsp. roasted cumin seeds. Salt and lime juice to taste.

Grind all the above ingredients to a paste and mix in lime juice and salt.

Sweet chutney

1 lime-sized ball of tamarind. 25 grams grated jaggery. 12 raisins. 1 tsp. cumin seeds. ½ tsp. garam masala. Salt and chilli powder to taste.

Cover tamarind with little water for 5 minutes, then squeeze out all the water. Grind the remaining ingredients to a paste and mix into the tamarind.

Coconut chutney

¼ coconut. 1 tblsp. urad dal. ½ tsp. mustard seeds. 1 cup beaten curds. 1 small bunch corriander leaves. 4 green chillies. 1-inch piece ginger. 1 tsp. cumin seeds. A few curry leaves. ½ tsp. garam masala. Salt to taste.

Heat 1 tblsp. ghee and fry dal, cumin seeds and curry leaves to a red colour and grind to a fine paste with the rest of the above ingredients with the exception of curds and mustard. Put the paste into the curds and milk well. Heat 1 tsp. ghee and add mustard, when they stop popping put over the chutney.

Coconut chutney

½ coconut. 25 grams roasted peanuts. 1 small onion. 4 green chillies. 1-inch piece ginger. Salt to taste. Lime juice and sugar to taste.

Grind all the above ingredients to a paste without adding water

Onion chutney

1 big onion. 2 red and 2 green chillies. 1 small piece ginger. A few pods tamarind. Salt and sugar to taste.

Grind all the above ingredients to a paste without adding water.

Garlic chutney

1 whole pod of garlic. 4 red chillies. 1 tsp. cumin seeds. 1 tblsp. corriander seeds. 1 small piece dry coconut. Salt to taste.

Roast all the above ingredients without garlic and grind to a fine paste without adding water. Store in airtight container. This chutney lasts for 15 days.

Raisin chutney

100 grams raisins. 4 red chillies. 1-inch piece ginger. Strained juice of 1 lime. 1 tsp. roasted and powdered cumin seeds. Salt to taste.

Grind all the above ingredients to a paste without adding water.

Til chutney

25 grams til. 1 small piece dry coconut. 20 flakes garlic. 1 tblsp. cumin seeds. 4 red chillies. Salt to taste.

Roast all the ingredients on a dry girdle and then grind to a paste without adding water. This chutney lasts for 15 to 20 days.

FARSHAN

Dry fruit kachori

250 grams maida. 1 tblsp. ghee. Salt to taste.

For filling......250 grams green peas, shelled and boiled. 25 grams each of walnuts, groundnuts, cashewnuts and raisins. 10 almonds and pistachios. 1 tblsp. charoli. 4 green chillies, minced. 1 small bunch finely sliced corriander leaves. $\frac{1}{4}$ tsp. sugar. $\frac{1}{2}$ finely grated coconut. 1 tblsp. each of ground cumin seeds and garam masala. Salt, chilli powder and lime juice to taste.

Mix together flour and salt, rub ghee and then add enough water to form a soft dough. Blanch and slice all the nuts finely. Mash the peas coarsely. Blend together all the filling ingredients. Divide the dough into small cups, stuff with filling, gather the edges together and form into round and smooth kachories or cutlets. Heat enough ghee for deep frying to smoking, lower the heat and put the kachories upside down so that it does not open out. Fry over a gentle heat to a golden brown colour. Drain and serve with chutney of your choice.

Peas Kachori

250 grams maida. 1 tblsp. ghee. Salt to taste.

For filling......250 grams boiled and coarsely mashed peas. Pinch of asafoetida. 4 flakes garlic. 1-inch piece ginger. A big handful of corriander leaves. $\frac{1}{2}$ finely grated coconut. 25 grams raisins. 1 tsp. each of ground cumin seeds and garam masala. $\frac{1}{4}$ tsp. each of mustard and cumin seeds. Salt and chilli powder to taste.

Mash garlic and ginger coarsely. Heat 2 tblsps. oil and toss in mustard and cumin seeds and asafoetida. When the seeds stop popping, add ginger and garlic and 4 minced green chillies and fry till the mixture starts changing colour. Put in rest of the filling ingredients. Mix well and remove from fire. Blend together maida and salt. Rub in ghee then add enough water to form a soft dough. Now prepare the kachories in the same way as shown in the above recipe.

Corn kachori

250 grams maida. 1 tblsp. ghee. Salt to taste.

For filling......4 tender corn cobs. 4 green chillies, minced. A big handful of corriander leaves. ½ tsp. turmeric powder. ½ tsp. each of ground cumin seeds and garam masala. ¼ finely grated coconut. Salt, lime juice and chilli powder to taste. A pinch of sugar.

Remove corn from cobs and boil. Mash coarsely and mix in all the filling ingredients. Mix together maida and salt. Rub in ghee and form soft dough, then form the kachories in the same way as shown in the recipe entitled "Dry fruit kachori"

Potato kachori

250 grams maida. 2 tblsps. sour curds. Pinch of soda bicarb. 2 tblsps. ghee. Salt to taste.

For filling......150 grams boiled and peeled potatoes. 50 grams boiled peas. 4 green chillies, minced. A big handful of sliced corriander leaves. 1

small piece ginger, minced. 1 tsp. each of corriander powder, ground cumin seeds and garam masala. Salt, chilli powder and lime juice to suit the taste. ¼ tsp. mustard seeds.

Mix together maida, salt and soda. Rub in ghee. add beaten curds along with enough warm water to form a soft dough. Heat 1 tblsp. oil and toss in the mustard seeds, add ginger and chillies and fry till soft. Put in the potatoes and peas and rest of the filling ingredients. Mix well and remove from fire. Divide the dough and the filling into equal number of portions and form the kachories in the same way as shown in the recipe entitled "Dry fruit kachories"

Dal kachori

250 grams maida. 1 cup curds. A pinch of soda bicarb. Salt to taste. For filling....... 100 grams urad dal. A few whole corriander seeds and peppercorns. ½ tsp. each of ground cumin seeds, corriander powder and garam masala. 1 tsp. sugar. Salt and chilli powder to taste.

Soak dal whole night in water. Grind coarsely next morning after draining out the water. Pound peppercorns and corriander seeds coarsely. Heat 2 tblsps. ghee and fry the dal after adding to it all the spices on a low fire till it is cooked and well-browned. Mix in the sugar and set aside Blend together maida, salt and soda. Rub in enough ghee till when pressed in hand it should hold. Mix in the curds and form a dough. Divide the dough and the filling into equal number of portions and then form the kachories in the same way as shown in the recipe entitled "Dry fruit kachories".

Sweet potato kachori

250 grams maida. 1 tblsp. ghee. Salt to taste.

For filling......250 grams boiled, peeled and coarsely mashed sweet potatoes. 3 green chillies, minced. A big handful of finely sliced corriander leaves. 1-inch piece ginger, minced. $\frac{1}{4}$ coconut, finely grated. 1 tsp. til, roasted. 25 grams raisins. 1 tsp. pomogranate seeds, crushed coarsely. Salt, lime juice and chilli powder to taste. $\frac{1}{2}$ tsp. each of ground cumin seeds and garam masala.

Mix together salt and maida. Rub in ghee and then add enough water to form a soft dough. Mix together all the filling ingredients. Divide the dough and the filling ingredients into equal number of portions and form kachories in the same way as shown in the recipe entitled "Dry fruit kachori".

Aluvadi

12 collocasia leaves. 1 cup urad or channa dal. 1 small ball tamarind. $\frac{1}{2}$ coconut, finely grated. 10 grams sugar. A big handful of finely sliced corriander leaves. 1-inch piece minced ginger. 4 green chillies, minced. Pinch of asafoetida. Salt and chilli powder to taste.

Cover tamarind with water for 5 minutes, then squeeze out the juice. Soak the dal whole night in water. Next morning, drain out the water and grind to a fine paste along with coconut.

Mix in the tamarind juice along with the rest of the above ingredients with the exception of leaves. The mixture of dal should be like a thin batter. If it is too thick, add water to obtain the right consistency. Clean the leaves with a wet rag. Remove the hard viens with a sharp knife taking care not to tear the leaf. Place a leaf upside down on the table and spread a thin layer of batter evenly over it. Spread another leaf on this and repeat the process. Do this until you have used up six leaves. Turn in the edges of the leaves on both the sides and roll up into a tight and neat roll. Tie the roll securely with thread and set aside. From the remaining leaves form another roll. Steam both the rolls together till tender. Remove from fire, cut into thin slices after cooling the rolls and deep fry till golden and crisp. Drain and serve with chutney of your choice.

Tomato Omelette

200 grams tomatoes, peeled and pured. 150 grams besan or gram flour. 5 green chillies, minced. 1 small bunch corriander leaves, minced. 1 tsp. til. $\frac{1}{2}$ tsp. turmeric powder. Salt and chilli powder to taste. 1 tblsp. sugar.

Mix together all the above ingredients to form a batter. If the batter is too thick add a little water to obtain the right consistency. Heat a girdle to smoking, lower the heat and grease it liberally with ghee. Put 2 tblsps. batter on it and spread it into a as thin round as you can. When the underside turns golden, put a little ghee around the edges and turn over. Remove from fire when both the sides turn golden colour-ed. Serve piping hot with fingerchips and chut-ney of your choice.

Masala Tikki

1½ cups gram flour. 4 green chillies. 4 flakes garlic. 1-inch piece ginger. 1 small bunch finely sliced corriander leaves. ½ cup rice flour. 1 tsp. turmeric powder. A pinch soda bicarb. 1 tsp. each of corriander powder and ground cumin seeds. Salt to taste.

For filling......¼ dry coconut. 2 tsps. each of poppy and sesame seeds. 1 tsp. garam masala. Salt and chilli powder to taste.

Roast to a golden colour coconut, khus khus and til and pound to a fine powder. Mix in the rest of the filling ingredients and set aside. Mix to-gether turmeric and rice flour then add enough water to form a thin batter. Grind together chillies, garlic and ginger. Mix the ground paste with gram flour, corriander leaves, soda, ground cumin seeds, corriander powder and soda. Mix in 4 cups water and place on a slow fire. Cook stirring frequently till the mixture turns thick and leaves the sides of the pan. Spread the mixture on a wet cloth which should be placed on the back of a thali. It should be spread in a rectan-gular shape of about one-eighth inch in thickness. Sprinkle the filling ingredients evenly on the surface of the rectangle, then quickly cover your hands with the wet side and fold the rectangle into half pressing it down firmly. Leave it till it turns cold, then remove from cloth, cut into pieces, dip in batter and deep fry to a golden brown colour. Drain and serve with chutney of your choice.

Dahi Vada

200 grams moong dal. 50 grams urad dal. 200 grams beaten curds. 4 green chillies. 1-inch piece ginger. Pinch asafoetida. Handful of finely sliced corriander leaves. ½ tsp. each of garam masala, ground cumin seeds and ground ajwain. 25 grams raisins. 10 pistachios and almonds.

Blanch and slice the nuts and raisins. Mix ajwain in 1 glass hot water and set aside. Soak the dals whole night in water. Next morning drain out the water and grind the dals to a paste. Mix in salt, asafoetida and finely sliced ginger and chillies. Form the dal mixture into small vadas around a few sliced nuts and raisins and deep fry to a golden colour. Drain and toss immediately into hot water. Set them aside for 15 minutes, then squeeze out the water gently pressing the vadas between the palms of both the hands. Put the badas in a serving dish. Pour curds over top. Sprinkle all the spices and corriander leaves on top before serving.

Chutney vada

250 grams moong dal. 25 grams raisins. 200 grams beaten curds. Salt to taste. A pinch baking powder.

For chutney......1 small ball tamarind. 1 small piece dry coconut. 25 grams grated jaggery. 1 tsp. til. 25 grams roasted ground nuts. 6 dates pitted and sliced. 1 tsp. each of garam masala and ground cumin seeds. Handful of finely sliced corriander leaves. 1 tsp. ground ajwain.

Put ajwain in 1 glass hot water and set aside. Cover tamarind with 1 cup water for 5 minutes and squeeze out the water. Roast coconut and til till brown and grind to a paste along with groundnuts, dates and jaggery. Heat tamarind, mix in garam masala, powdered cumin seeds, salt and ground paste and cook till quite thick. Remove from fire and set aside. Soak the dal whole night in water. Next morning, drain out the water and grind to a smooth paste. Mix in raisins, salt and baking powder. Form into round vadas and deep fry to a golden colour. Drain and put immediately in hot water. Leave them for 15 minutes, then gently squeeze out the water by pressing them between the palms of both the hands. Put them in a serving dish. Pour chutney on top, then pour curds. Sprinkle chilli powder and corriander leaves on top before serving.

Urad Dal Bajia

250 grams urad dal. 1 small bunch corriander leaves. 1-inch piece ginger. 4 green chillies. 4 flakes garlic. 1 small onion. 1 tsp. coarsely powdered cumin seeds. Salt and chilli powder to to taste.

Soak dal for a few hours in water. Drain out

the water and grind to a smooth paste. Grind
the remaining ingredients to a coarse paste and
mix into the dal. Form into small balls and
deep fry to a golden brown colour. Drain and
serve with chutney of your choice.

Channa Dal Bajia

250 grams channa dal. 4 green chillies. 1 small
bunch corriander leaves. 1 tsp. each of cumin
and coarsely pounded anise seeds. Pinch each
of asafoetida and soda bicarb. Salt to taste. 1-
inch piece ginger, minced.

Soak the dal in water for 5 hours. Drain out
the water and grind to a coarse paste along with
chillies, corriander leaves, onion and ginger.
Mix in the rest of the above ingredients. Form
into small balls and deep fry to a golden brown
colour. Drain and serve with chutney of your
choice.

Vegetable Vada

250 grams urad dal. 1 tsp. ground cumin seeds.
4 green chillies, minced. 1-inch piece ginger,
minced. 1 small onion, minced. 1 small bunch
finely sliced corriander leaves. 100 grams mixed
vegetables like carrots, cauliflower, peas and
frenchbeans. A pinch asafoetida. Salt to suit
the taste. 1 tsp. garam masala.

Steam all the vegetables and mash to a paste.
Soak dal whole night in water. Next morning,
drain out the water and grind to a paste. Mix
V. W. G.—4

in the rest of the above ingredients and knead to a smooth mixture. Form into small balls and deep fry to a golden brown colour. Drain and serve with chutney of your choice.

Dal Handva

500 grams rice. 1 handful each of urad and toovar dal. 2 handfuls of channa dal. 1 glass sour buttermilk. 1-inch piece ginger. 4 flakes garlic. A pinch of asafoetida. 1 small bunch corriander leaves. 6 green chillies. 1 tsp. oil mixed with $\frac{1}{4}$ tsp. soda. $\frac{1}{2}$ tsp. each of fenugreek and mustard seed. A few curry leaves. $\frac{1}{2}$ tsp. cumin seeds. 1 tsp. turmeric powder. 2 tblsps. til. Salt and chilli powder to taste.

Wash and soak the rice and dals separately for 6 hours. Drain and grind the rice and the dals together coarsely. Put in buttermilk and set aside for 10 hours. Grind together ginger, garlic and chillies and mix into the batter along with soda and corriander leaxes. Heat 4 tblsps. oil and put in asafoetida, curry leaves, fenugreek, cumin and mustard seeds. When the seeds stop popping and the mixture turns red, put in the spices and salt and batter. Now take a greased baking dish and put in the batter. Level the surface and sprinkle til on top. Cover tightly. Place a girdle or tava over the lid, put live coals in it and cook over a slow fire for 20 minutes or until the top turns biscuit coloured. Cut into slices and serve with sweet chutney. If you like you can also bake it in a moderate oven.

Vegetable Handva

2 cups rice. 2 cups channa dal. 1 cup toovar dal. $\frac{1}{2}$ cup each of moong and urad dal. 250 grams coarsely ground peas. 100 grams each of finely sliced marrow or pumpkin and cauliflower. 1 tsp. turmeric powder. $\frac{1}{4}$ tsp. soda bicarb blended in 1 tsp. oil. 4 tblsps. sour curds. A big pinch asafoetida. 5 green chillies. 1 small bunch corriander leaves. 1 tsp. sugar. 1 tsp. mustard seeds. 2 tblsps. til. Salt and chilli powder to taste.

Wash and soak the rice and dals separately for 6 hours. Drain and grind the rice and the dals together coarsely. Mix in the sour curds along with enough hot water to form a thick batter. Cover and set aside for 10 hours. Grind together ginger and chillies and mix into the batter along with salt all the vegetables and corriander leaves. Heat 6 tblsps. oil and toss in the mustard seeds and asafoetida. When the seeds stop popping, put into the handva. Put the mixture in a greased baking dish, level the surface and sprinkle til on top. Bake in the same manner as shown in the above recipe.

Doodhi Handva

3 cups rice. $\frac{1}{4}$ cup each of moong, urad, channa and toovar dal. 2 cups sour curds. 1 small doodhi, peeled and finely grated. $\frac{1}{4}$ tsp. soda bicarb mixed with 1 tsp. oil. $\frac{1}{4}$ tsp. each of mustard, cumin and fenugreek seeds. 5 green chillies. 4 flakes garlic. 1 big piece ginger. 1 small bunch corriander leaves. Salt and chilli powder to taste.

Wash and soak the rice and dals separately for 6 hours. Drain out the water and grind to a thick paste. Mix in the curds and set aside for 10 hours. Grind ginger, chillies, corriander leaves and garlic and mix into the dals. Squeeze out the water from doodhi and mix inside. Mix thoroughly and put in the rest of the above ingredients with the exception of mustard, cumin and fenugreek seeds. Put the mixture in a greased baking dish then heat 4 tblsps. oil and toss in mustard, fenugreek and cumin seeds. When the mixture turns brown, put over the batter. Bake gram flour. Milk of 1 coconut. 1 tsp. each of entitled "Dal Handva".

Cauliflower Handva

1 kilo cauliflower. $\frac{1}{2}$ kilo green peas. 4 tblsps. gram flour. Milk of 1 coconut. 1 tsp. each of dhaniajeera powder and garam masala and turmeric powder. 1-inch piece ginger. 2 medium onions, finely sliced 1 bunch corriander leaves. 1 tblsp. sugar. Strained juice of 1 lime. 7 green chillies. Salt and chilli powder to taste.

Boil cauliflower and peas in water till tender and dry. Fry onions in little ghee till soft. Grind smooth mixture. Divide potatoes and the filling to a paste. Mix together all the above ingredients then put in a well-greased baking dish. Bake in the same way as shown in the recipe entitled "Dal Handva".

Papaya Tikki

500 grams potatoes, boiled and peeled. 2 small

slices of bread, soaked in water and squeezed dry. 1 cup bread crumbs.

For filling......1 small raw papaya, peeled and grated. 100 grams shelled green peas. 1-inch piece ginger. 1 big tomato, peeled and sliced. 2 green chillies. 1 small bunch corriander leaves. ¼ tsp. garam masala. ¼ tsp. turmeric powder. Salt and chilli powder to taste.

Grind ginger, chillies and corriander leaves. Heat 2 tblsps. oil, add tomatoes and all the spices and cook till soft. Mix in the rest of the filling ingredients. Cover tightly and cook without adding water till the vegetables are soft and dry. Remove from fire and set aside. Mix potatoes with bread and salt and knead to a smooth mixture. Divide the potato and filling into equal numbers of portions. Form the potato mixture into round cutlets around the filling, roll in crumbs and deep fry to a golden brown colour. Drain and serve with chutney of your choice.

Cabbage Tikki

500 grams potatoes, boiled and peeled. 2 small slices of bread, soaked in water and squeezed dry. 1 cup bread crumbs. Salt to taste.

For filling......100 grams each of cabbage and green peas. 2 tblsps. grated coconut. A handful sliced corriander leaves. ½-inch piece ginger, minced 2 green chillies, minced. 1 tsp. sugar. ¼ tsp. turmeric powder. 1 tsp. ground cumin seeds. Salt, chilli powder and lime juice to taste.

Shred the cabbage and shell the peas. Steam the vegetables. Mash the peas coarsely and mix with all the filling ingredients. Mix together potatoes and bread and salt and knead to a smooth mixture. Divide potatoes and the filling into equal number of portions. Form the potatoes into smooth and round cutlets and roll in crumbs deep fry to a golden brown colour. Drain and serve with chutney of your choice.

Dal Tikki

500 grams potatoes, boiled and peeled. 2 small slices of bread soaked in water and squeezed dry. 1 cup bread crumbs. Salt to taste.

For filling......200 grams green toovar. 1 small bunch corriander leaves. 1 tsp. roasted and powdered cumin seeds. 1-inch piece ginger. 2 green chillies. 2 tblsps. grated coconut. 1 tsp. sugar. $\frac{1}{4}$ tsp. turmeric powder. Salt and lime juice to taste.

Boil the dal in little water till soft, then grind with all the filling ingredients to a smooth paste. Mix potatoes with bread and salt and knead into a smooth mixture, now form into tikkis as shown in the above recipe.

Corn Tikki

500 grams potatoes, boiled and peeled. 2 small slices of bread, soaked in water and squeezed dry. 1 cup bread crumbs. Salt to taste.

For filling......2 tender corn cobs. 2 green chillies, minced. Handful of sliced corriander leaves. 25 grams fried and sliced raisins. ½-inch piece ginger, minced. ¼ tsp. each of garam masala and ground cumin seeds. A few fried and chopped cashewnuts. 1 tsp. sugar 1 tblsp. grated coconut. Salt and chilli powder to taste.

Remove corn from cobs, boil and drain and mash coarsely then mix with all the filling ingredients. Mix potatoes and bread and salt and knead to a smooth mixture. Now make the tikkis in the same way as shown in the recipe entitled "Cabbage Tikki."

Corn Rolls

12 tender collocasia or arvi leaves. 4 fresh corn cobs. ¼ coconut. 1 tsp. garam masala. 1-inch piece ginger. 4 flakes garlic. 4 green chillies. 1 tblsp. sugar. 1 small bunch corriander leaves. 1 lime-sized ball of tamarind. 4 tblsps. rice flour. Salt and chilli powder to taste.

Cover tamarind with water for 5 minutes and then squeeze out the juice. Remove corn from cobs and grind to a paste along with all the above ingredients with the exception of flour and leaves. Mix the paste into tamarind and set aside. Put salt and enough water in flour to form a thin batter. Clean the leaves with a wet rag. Remove the hard veins with a sharp knife taking care not to tear the leaves. The mixture of corn should be like a thin batter. If it is thick, add water to obtain the right consistency. Place a leaf upside down on the table and spread a thin layer of corn mixture evenly over it. Spread another leaf over it and repeat the process. Do this until you have used up six leaves. Turn in the edges of the leaves on both the sides and roll up into a tight and neat roll. Tie the roll securely with a thread and set aside. From the remaining leaves form another roll. Steam both the rolls together for half an hour. Remove from fire, cut into thin slices, dip in batter and deep fry till crisp and golden. Drain and serve with chutney of your choice.

Khakhada

250 grams flour. 1 tblsp. each of coarsely pounded cumin seeds and peppercorns. Salt to taste.

Mix together all the above ingredients and then add enough water to form a stiff dough. Divide the dough into small balls and roll out each ball into a chapati with the help of a little dry flour. Bake each chapati lightly on both the sides. Apply ghee liberally to each side of chapati and stack them one over the other and set aside for a couple of hours. Then re-roast chapati over the girdle with the help of a piece of cloth till crisp and biscuit coloured. Cool and store in airtight tins.

Green channa chivda

500 grams dry green channa. 100 grams channa dal. 100 grams groundnuts. 1tblsp. sugar. 1 tblsp. roasted and coarsely pounded cumin seeds. A few curry leaves. A few green chillies. $\frac{1}{4}$ dry coconut, sliced finely.

Soak channa and dal separately whole night in water. Next morning, drain out the water and dry them for one hour. Mix in salt and deep fry them separately over a slow fire till crisp and golden. Drain and set aside. Also fry nuts and coconut to a golden colour. Prick chillies at a few places and deep fry with curry leaves till crisp. Drain thoroughly and mix all the above ingredients. Cool thoroughly and store in airtight container.

Potato chivda

500 grams potatoes. 100 grams each of peanuts and cashewnuts. ¼ dry coconut sliced finely. A few curry leaves. 4 green chillies. 1 tblsp. poppy seeds and til. 25 grams raisins. 1 tblsp. roasted cumin seeds. 1 tblsp. sugar. Salt to taste.

Peel the potatoes and cut into fine straws. Soak in cold water for 1 hour, drain and squeeze out all the water then deep fry a little at a time till they start changing colour. Drain, cool thoroughly, mix in salt and fry once again till crisp and golden. Drain and set aside. Also fry the nuts and raisins and coconut to a golden colour. Prick chillies at a few places and fry with curry leaves till crisp. Drain and put into the potato straws. Fry poppy seeds and til in very little ghee to a light golden colour. Mix with all the above ingredients, cool nicely and store in airtight tin.

Corn chivda

6 corn cobs. 100 grams peanuts. 200 grams potatoes, ¼ dry coconut, sliced finely. 1 tblsp. each of til, sugar, turmeric powder and ground cumin seeds. A few curry leaves. Salt and chilli pow-

der to taste. 25 grams raisins. Salt to suit the taste. Remove corn from cobs. Melt 2 tblsps. ghee in a heavy-bottomed pan put in corn to cover the bottom, cover tightly and place over moderate fire for 5 to 10 minutes or till the corn stops popping and turns crisp. Remove from fire. Peel potatoes, cut into fine straws and soak in cold water for 1 hour. Squeeze out all the water and deep fry till they start changing colour. Drain, cool thoroughly, mix in salt and deep fry once again till crisp and golden. Drain and set aside. Also fry peanuts and coconut to a brown colour. Fry curry leaves till crisp and remove from fire. Roast til lightly and mix with all the above ingredients. Cool and store in airtight tin.

Fried dal

Clean and soak either moong or channa dal whole night in water. Next morning, drain out the water completely and wipe with cloth to remove excess moisture, mix in salt and deep fry a little at a time till crisp and golden. Drain thoroughly, cool and store in airtight tin. When wanted for use, mix in a little chilli powder and garam masala. Also add some minced onion and corriander leaves and lime juice. Mix well before serving.

VEGETABLES

Dudhi muthia

250 grams gram flour. 50 grams flour. 250 grams pumpkin or marrow, peeled or grated. 1 small bunch corriander leaves. 4 green chillies. ½ tsp. turmeric powder. 1-inch piece ginger. 2 tblsps. oil ¼ tsp. sugar 1 tsp. corriander powder. 1 tsp. ground cumin seeds. A pinch asafoetida. ¼ tsp. mustard seeds. Salt and chilli powder to taste. Grind corriander leaves, chillies and ginger to a paste and mix with all the above ingredients with the exception of mustard seeds and asafoetida. Knead to a smooth mixture, do not add water. If the mixture does not form a dough add a little sour curds. Form the mixture into thin and long rolls and steam for about half an hour. Remove from fire, cool and cut into thin slices. Heat 2 tblsps. oil and add asafoetida and mustard seeds, when the seeds stop popping, put in the pieces of muthia and fry over a slow fire till they are slightly brown. Sprinkle chopped corriander leaves and a little grated coconut on top before serving.

Muli Muthia

500 grams finely grated white radishes. 300 grams coarse rava-like wheat flour. 2 tblsps. gram flour. 2 tblsps. sour curds. ½ tsp. turmeric powder. 1-inch piece ginger. 4 green chillies. 1 small bunch corriander leaves. A pinch asafoetida. 1 tsp. mustard seeds. 4 tblsps. oil. 2 tblsps. grated coconut. Salt and chilli powder to taste.

Grind ginger, chillies and corriander leaves to a paste. Mix with all the above ingredients with the exception of asafoetida, mustard seeds and coconut. Now prepare and serve in the same way as Dudhi muthia.

Cabbage Muthia

500 grams cabbage, finely grated. 100 grams gram flour. 100 grams flour. 50 grams jowar flour. 1 small piece dry coconut. 1 tblsp. til. 5 green chillies. 1 small bunch corriander leaves. 2 tblsps. grated coconut. 1 tsp. each of turmeric powder and mustard seeds. Pinch of asafoetida. 1-inch piece ginger. 1 tsp. garam masala. Salt, sugar, lime juice and chilli powder to taste.

Roast and grind til and dry coconut. Grind green chillies, ginger and corriander leaves to a paste. Mix together all the above ingredients with the exception of mustard, grated coconut and asafoetida. Now add enough water to flour mixture to form a soft dough. Now prepare and serve in the same way as dudhi muthia.

Methi Muthia

1 big bunch fenugreek leaves, cleaned and sliced finely. 4 flakes garlic. 4 green chillies. $\frac{1}{2}$-inch piece ginger. Handful of corriander leaves. 1 tsp. ground cumin seeds. 1 cup coarse rava-like flour. 1 cup besan. 1 tsp. turmeric powder. 2 tblsps. sour curds. 3 tblsps. oil. A big pinch sugar. 1 tsp. mustard seeds. A pinch asafoetida. 2 tblsps. grated coconut. Salt and chilli powder to taste.

Grind ginger, chillies and garlic to a paste. Mix together all the above ingredients with the exception of mustard, asafoetida, coconut and corriander leaves. Add very little water and form a soft dough, then prepare and serve in the same way as dudhi muthia.

Undia

1 small bunch corriander leaves. 4 green chillies. 1-inch piece ginger. 4 flakes garlic. 1 tsp. cumin seeds. ¼ tsp. ajwain. ¼ cup groundnuts. 2 tblsps. roasted and pounded til. ½ coconut, finely grated. 1 tsp. garam masala. 1 tblsp. sugar. 250 grams surti papadi. 12 baby potatoes, peeled. 150 grams tomatoes, blanched and sliced. 5 small brinjals. 2 sweet potatoes. ½ cup shelled green toovar pulse. 2 small raw guavas. 2 small raw bananas. 2 small carrots.

For muthia......125 grams gram flour. 1 big bunch fenugreek leaves, cleaned and sliced finely. 1 big onion, minced. 1 flake garlic, crushed. Buttermilk. A pinch asafoetida. 2 green chillies. 1 tblsp. oil. Salt to taste.

Mix all the muthia ingredients together with the exception of buttermilk, then add enough buttermilk to form soft and pliable dough. Form the dough into small oblong-shaped balls and steam for half an hour, or till done. Remove from fire and set aside. Peel and cut bananas, sweet potatoes, guavas and carrots into pieces. Cut brinjals into four halfway through. String papadis. Soak groundnuts in water for half an hour and then remove peels. Powder ajwain and cumin seeds. Heat 4 tblsps. oil and add asafoetida and tomatoes and all the ground spices, and chillies, ginger and garlic after grinding them. Fry briefly, then add tomatoes and sugar and cook till soft. Put in all the vegetables, mix well, then put in the peanuts and half of grated coconut and toovar pulse. Cover tightly and cook without adding water over a slow fire till the vegetables are almost done. Mix in the til and arrange muthias on top. Cover and cook once again till the vegetables are done. Serve hot decorated with corriander leaves and remaining grated coconut.

Potato dhokli

500 grams val papadi. 4 green chillies. 1 tsp. turmeric powder. $\frac{1}{2}$ tsp. garam masala. 1 lime-sized ball of tamarind. 2 tblsps. grated jaggery. Handful of sliced corriander leaves. 1 small onion, finely sliced. 2 flakes garlic, sliced. 1-inch piece ginger. Salt and chilli powder to taste.

For dhokli......250 grams wheat flour. 150 grams potatoes, boiled, peeled and mashed. 25 grams gram flour. 50 grams oil. $\frac{1}{2}$ tsp. each of ground cumin seeds and ajwain. Salt to taste.

Mix together all the dhokli ingredients and knead to a smooth dough. Do not add water. Grind ginger and chillies to a paste. Put tamarind in 1 cup water for 5 minutes and then squeeze out the water. Dissolve jaggery in tamarind water. Divide the dhokli dough into 4 equal portions and roll out each piece into a round circle or puri. Cut the circle into long strips and each strip into pieces. Heat 4 tblsps. oil and add all the ground spices, fry briefly, then add the papadis and fry for 5 minutes. Cover with water and cook till the papadis are almost done, then put in the dhokli pieces and continue cooking till the vegetables and dhokli are done. Put in the tamarind and cook for 5 more minutes. Remove from fire and set aside. Fry sliced onion and garlic in 1 tblsp. oil till brown and put into the vegetables. Sprinkle corriander leaves on top before serving.

Gavar dhokli

250 grams gavar or cluster beans. A pinch asafoetida. A big pinch fenugreek seeds. $\frac{1}{2}$ tsp. mustard seeds. $\frac{1}{2}$ tsp. garam masala. 4 green chillies. 1 small bunch corriander leaves. 4 flakes garlic. 1 tblsp. grated jaggery. 1 tblsp. grated coconut. 2 to 3 tblsps. tamarind juice. Salt and chilli powder to taste.

For dhokli......$\frac{1}{2}$ cup gram flour. 1 tblsp. rice flour. 2 tblsps. oil. Salt to taste.

Mix all the dhokli ingredients and form a dough with very little water. Roll out the dough into a round chapati. Cut the chapati into strips and each strip into small pieces. Grind garlic, chillies and corriander leaves to a paste. Heat 2 tblsps. oil and put in asafoetida, mustard and fenugreek seeds. When the mixture turns brown, add gavar all the spices, salt, chilli powder and ground paste and fry for 5 minutes. Cover with water and cook till the gavar is almost done, put in the dhokli pieces and continue cooking till both the gavar and the dhokli pieces are done. Put in tamarind and jaggery and cook over a slow fire for 5 minutes.   Serve decorated with grated coconut and corriander leaves.

Rice dhokli

250 grams baby potatoes, peeled. 250 grams green peas, shelled. 1 tsp. mustard seeds. Pinch of asafoetida. 1-inch piece ginger, minced. 4 green chillies, minced. 1 tsp. turmeric powder. 1 tsp. corriander powder. 2 tblsps. grated coconut. 100 grams tomatoes, blanched and sliced.   A few curry leaves. Salt and chilli powder to taste. 6 flakes garlic.

For dhokli......250 grams rice flour 3 green chillies. 1 small bunch sliced corriander leaves. 1 tsp. ground cumin seeds. Salt and chilli powder to taste.

Grind chillies and corriander leaves to a paste and mix with flour with all the dhokli ingredients Make a thin batter of flour with water and place over a slow fire. Cook till the mixture turns thick and leaves the sides of the vessel. Put in a greased thali, set aside to turn cold, then cut into small pieces. Heat 3 tblsps. oil and add asafoetida and mustard seeds, when the seeds stop popping, add ginger, garlic flakes and all the spices and fry briefly.   Put in the tomatoes, chillies and curry leaves and cook till soft. Put in peas and potatoes, fry for 5 minutes and then cover with water. Cook till the vegetables are almost done, then put in the dhokli pieces and if you like a teaspoon of sugar, continue cooking till the vegetables are done.   Serve decorated with coconut and corriander leaves.

Sago khichdai

1 cup sabudana. ½ cup roasted and coarsely powdered groundnuts. 1 tsp. pounded cumin seeds. 2 green chillies, minced. Salt to taste. A few sprigs of corriander leaves.

Wash sabudana nicely in water and then drain out the water. Heat 3 tblsps. oil and add chillies, fry briefly then put in the rest of the ingredients with the exception of corriander leaves. Cover and cook over a slow fire till done.

Batata poha

200 grams fine poha. 50 grams each of baby potatoes and shelled peas. 1 medium onion, finely sliced. 1 tsp. powdered cumin seeds. ½ tsp. mustard seeds. A pinch of asafoetida. ½ tsp. turmeric powder. A few sprigs corriander leaves. ½ tsp sugar. 2 tblsps. grated coconut. 2 green chillies, minced. 1 inch piece ginger, minced. Salt, chilli powder and lime juice to taste.

Wash the poha in water and then drain out the water nicely. Heat 3 tblsps. oil and toss in mustard and asafoetida, when the seeds stop popping, put in all the spices and fry briefly. Add onion, ginger and chillies and fry till soft and almond-coloured. Put in potatoes, peas and sugar. Cover and cook over a slow fire without adding water till the vegetables are cooked. Put in the poha, mix well and continue cooking for 10 more minutes. Remove from fire, sprinkle lime juice on top and serve decorated with corriander leaves and coconut.

Sabudana and potatoes khichadi

75 grams sabudana. 250 grams potatoes, peeled and sliced. 250 grams roasted and pounded groundnuts. 2 green chillies, minced. 2 red chillies. 1 tsp. each of sugar and coarsely pounded cumin seeds. 2 tblsps. grated coconut. A few sprigs corriander leaves. 1 small piece ginger, minced. ½ tsp. turmeric powder. Salt and chilli powder to taste.

Wash and soak sabudana in water for 15 minutes and then drain out the water. Heat 2 tblsps. oil, add whole red chillies, fry till brown and then put in ginger and green chillies and fry till soft. Put in all the spices and salt and fry briefly, add potatoes and fry for 5 minutes. Put in 1 cup water and sugar and cook till the potatoes are half done, then add sabudana and groundnuts and continue cooking till potatoes are done. Remove from fire and sprinkle lime juice on top. Serve garnished with sprigs of corriander leaves and coconut.

Shingh poha

250 grams fine poha. 100 grams roasted and coarsely pounded groundnuts. 100 grams potatoes. 1 medium onion, cut finely. 2 green chillies minced. ½ tsp. turmeric powder. 1 tsp. mustard seeds. Pinch of asafoetida. 1 tsp. ground cumin seeds. 1 tblsp. roasted til. 2 tblsps. grated coconut. Handful of sliced corriander leaves. Lime juice, salt and chilli powder to taste.

Wash poha in water and squeeze out the water.

Peel and cut the potatoes into fine straws. Heat 2 tblsps. oil and add mustard seeds and asafoetida. When the seeds stop popping, put in the remaining spices and salt and fry briefly. Add onions and chillies and fry till soft. Put in potatoes, fry for 5 minutes, then cover tightly and cook till the potatoes are cooked. Now add groundnuts, til and poha and cook for 10 minutes. Remove from fire and sprinkle lime juice on top. Serve decorated with coconut and corriander leaves.

Stuffed karela

250 grams bittergourds. 2½ tblsps. gram flour 1 tblsp. dhania jeera. 1 tsp. turmeric powder. 2 tblsps. oil. Salt, sugar and lime juice to suit the taste.

Make a slit halfway through in the centre of each bittergourd and sprinkle liberally with salt. Set aside for 4 hours, then squeeze out all the water, wash nicely in 4 to 5 changes of water, squeezing out the water nicely after each wash. Now mix together the rest of the above ingredients and fill into the slits. Tie with thread, then heat 4 tblsps. oil in a heavy-bottomed pan and put in the bittergourds, fry gently for 5 minutes, then cover the pan tightly and cook over a slow fire till the gourds are done. Serve hot.

Batata vangi nu shak

250 grams potatoes, peeled and sliced. 1 big brinjal, sliced into thin and long slices. 2 big tomatoes, peeled and sliced. 1 tsp. each of sugar and dhania

jeera powder. ½ tsp. each of turmeric powder and garam masala. Salt and chilli powder to taste.

Heat 3 tblsps. oil and put in tomatoes, all the spices and sugar and cook till the tomatoes are soft. Put in potatoes and brinjals and fry for 5 minutes. Pour in 1½ cups water and cook till the vegetables are done. Serve decorated with corriander leaves.

Brinjals fried

1 big brinjal. 1 tsp. dhaniajeera powder. ½ tsp. garam masala. ½ tsp. each of pepper powder and mango powder. Salt and chilli powder to taste.

Cut the brinjal into half and each half into 3 slices. Make fine slits on the cut surface of each slice and then mix all the above spices and rub nicely on the slits. Heat 4 tblsps. oil and put the brinjals cut side down into the pan. Cover tightly and cook over a slow fire turning them occasionally till they are soft. Serve hot.

Stuffed brinjals

8 small brinjals. 1 medium potato. ¼ coconut. ½-inch piece ginger. 2 green chillies. 1 tsp. gram flour. 1 tsp. dhania jeera powder. ½ tsp. garam masala. ½ tsp. turmeric powder. Handful of corriander leaves. 1 tblsp. roasted til. 25 grams each of raisins and roasted and pounded groundnuts. Lime juice, salt and chilli powder to taste.

Wash and wipe the brinjals and cut into four halfway through. Peel and mince the potato. Grate the coconut finely. Slice the raisins. Grind together ginger, chillies and corriander leaves and mix with all the above ingredients with the exception of brinjals, then stuff the mixture nicely into each brinjal. Heat 4 tblsps. oil and fry the brinjals gently for 5 minutes. Cover tightly and cook without adding water till the brinjals are done.

Stuffed capsicums

250 grams big capsicums. 2 big potatoes, boiled, peeled and mashed. 4 flakes garlic. 1 small piece ginger. 4 green chillies. 1 small bunch corriander leaves. 1 tsp. dhania jeera powder. ½ tsp. each of turmeric powder and garam masala. Salt, lime juice and chilli powder to taste.

Wash and wipe the capsicums, then cut each into half, halfway through. Grind chillies, ginger, garlic and corriander leaves with potatoes. Add spices lime juice and salt and mix thoroughly. Stuff the mixture nicely into each capsicum. Heat 3 tblsps. oil and put in the capsicums, fry gently for 5 minutes, then cover and cook over a slow fire without adding water till the capsicums are done. Serve hot.

Corn in curds

2 tender corn cobs. 1 cup beaten curds. 1 tsp. cumin seeds. 1-inch piece ginger. 4 green chillies. A few sprigs corriander leaves. 1 tsp. dhania jeera powder. ½ tsp. each of garam masala and turmeric powder. Salt and chilli powder to taste.

Grind together chillies and ginger. Beat curds with 1 cup water till smooth. Grate the corn finely. Heat 3 tblsps. oil and add cumin seeds when they stop popping, put in the corn and fry for 5 minutes, stirring it continuously. Put in all the spices, salt and ginger paste. Mix well and then put in the curds. Cover and cook till the raw smell of corn disappears. Sprinkle corriander leaves on top before serving.

Makka nu shak

3 tender corn cobs. 1 medium onion, minced. 2 flakes garlic, ground coarsely. 3 to 4 tblsps. tamarind juice. 2 tblsps. grated coconut 2 green chillies minced. ½ tsp. each of mustard seeds and turmeric powder. 2 cloves. 1 tsp. sugar. A few sprigs corriander leaves. 1 tsp. dhania jeera powder. Salt and chilli powder to taste.

Grate the corn finely. Heat 2 tblsps. oil and fry onion and garlic till soft. Add all the ground spices and salt and fry briefly. Add corn and fry for 5 minutes, stirring all the time. Put in sugar and tamarind juice and cook over a slow fire till the raw smell disappears. Remove from fire and set aside. Heat 1 tblsp. oil and put in mustard seeds and cloves. When the seeds stop popping, add chillies and fry briefly, put over the corn. Serve hot decorated with corriander leaves and coconut.

Stuffed chillies

100 grams long and thick green chillies. ½ cup coarsely pounded roasted groundnuts. 1 small piece dry coconut. 1 tsp. sugar. 1 small onion. 2 flakes garlic. 1 small piece ginger. Handful of

corriander leaves. 1 tsp. til. ½ tsp. turmeric powder. ½ tsp. each of ground cumin seeds and whole mustard seeds. Salt, lime juice and chilli powder to taste.

Roast til and coconut and powder. Grind onion, ginger, garlic and corriander leaves to a paste. Mix with all the above ingredients with the exception of mustard seeds and chillies. Wash and wipe the chillies and cut each into half in the centre halfway through. Stuff with the coconut and groundnut mixture. Heat 4 tblsps. oil and toss in mustard seeds, when they stop popping, put in the chillies. Cover tightly and cook over a slow fire till the chillies are done.

Mirchi nu shak

125 grams thick and long green chillies. 50 grams roasted and pounded groundnuts. 50 grams dry coconut. 2 tblsps. poppy seeds. 1 tblsp. roasted til. ½ tsp. each of cumin and mustard seeds. ½ tsp. turmeric powder 50 grams grated jaggery. Salt, lime juice and chilli powder to taste.

Cut chillies into long pieces slantwise. Roast coconut and poppy seeds and grind together with til. Heat 3 tblsps. oil and add mustard and cumin seeds, when the seeds stop popping, add chillies and all the spices and salt and cook till the chillies are soft. Put in the jaggery and continue cooking till it melts and the mixture turns thick. Mix in the rest of the above ingredients and remove from fire. This shak lasts for 1 week.

Kobi nu shak

500 grams cabbage, finely shreded. 50 grams roasted and pounded groundnuts. 25 grams sliced raisins. 1-inch piece ginger, ground. 2 to 3 chillies, ground. A few sprigs corriander leaves. 1 tsp. garam masala. ½ tsp. each of mustard seeds, turmeric powder and dhania jeera powder. Salt, chilli powder and lime juice to taste. 1 tsp. sugar.

Heat 2 tblsps. oil and add mustard seeds, when the seeds stop popping add all the spices and fry briefly. Put in cabbage with the rest of the above ingredients with exception of lime juice and corriander leaves. Cover tightly and cook over a slow fire without adding water till the cabbage is done. Remove from fire, sprinkle lime juice and corriander leaves on top before serving.

Kachi kerry nu shak

1 medium raw mango, peeled and sliced. 50 grams grated jaggery. A big pinch fenugreek seeds. A pinch asafoetida. 2 red chillies. ¼ tsp. turmeric powder. ¼ tsp. garam masala. Salt and chilli powder to taste.

Heat 1 tblsp. oil and put in asafoetida, fenugreek seeds and whole chillies and fry till the mixture turns brown. Add mangoes, salt, chilli and turmeric powder. Cover and cook over a slow fire till the mango is soft. Put in jaggery and cook till the jaggery melts and the mixture turns thick. Sprinkle garam masala on top before serving.

Pukki kerry nu shak No. 1

6 ripe and small mangoes, peeled. 4 red chillies.
½ tsp. cumin seeds. ½ tsp. turmeric powder. 25
grams grated jaggery. 2 to 3 tblsps. tamarind
juice. ½ tsp. mustard seeds. 2 flakes garlic. 1 small
onion.   Salt and chilli powder to taste.

Grind chillies, cumin seeds, garlic and onion to a
paste. Heat 2 tblsps. oil and add mustard, when
the seeds stop popping, put in the ground paste
and fry till the raw smell disappears. Put in the
mangoes, jaggery, 1 cup water and tamarind juice
and cook till the gravy turns thick.

Pukki kerry nu shak no. 2.

6 small ripe mangoes, peeled.   ½ tsp. mustard
seeds. A pinch of hing. ½ tsp. turmeric powder.
1 tsp. garam masala. Sugar, salt and chilli powder to state.

Heat 1 tblsp. oil and add mustard and asafoetida, when the seeds stop popping, add all the
spices with the exception of garam masala. Put
in the mangoes, sugar salt and ½ cup water. Cook
over a slow fire till the gravy turns thick.
Sprinkle garam masala on top before serving.

Padval ka ravaiya

250 gram big padvals. ½ coconut. 1-inch piece
ginger. 4 green chillies. 1 tsp. dhaniajeera powder. Pinch asafoetida.   Handful of corriander
leaves. ½ tsp. turmeric powder. 1 tsp. sugar. Salt
and chilli powder to taste.

Peel padvals. Grind the rest of the ingredients to a paste and mix in 2 tsp. of oil. Cut the padvals halfway through in the centre and scoop out the inner pith, then fill with the filling and tie with a thread. Heat 4 tblsps. and put in the padvals, cook over a slow fire without adding water till the padvals are done. Sprinkle lime juice and corriander leaves on top before serving.

Padval nu shak

250 grams padvals. $\frac{1}{2}$ coconut. 1-inch piece ginger. 4 green chillies. 1 small ball tamarind. 1 medium onion, finely sliced. $\frac{1}{2}$ tsp. turmeric powder. 1 tsp. each of sugar and dhaniajeera powder. $\frac{1}{2}$ tsp. mustard seeds. 2 red chillies. A few curry leaves. A few sprigs corriander leaves. Salt to taste.

Peel the padvals and cut into half halfway through. Remove the inner pith and discard. Cover tamarind with water for 5 minutes and then squeeze out the juice. Grind the coconut, ginger, green chillies and sugar. Mix in dhaniajeera powder, little turmeric powder and salt and stuff into each padval. Tie with thread. Heat 2 tblsps. oil and toss in mustard seeds, curry leaves and red chillies. When the mixture turns brown, put in onions, turmeric and salt and cook till raw smell disappears. Put in the padvals and fry gently for 5 minutes. Put in tamarind water. Cover tightly and cook over a slow fire without adding water till the padvals are done. Serve decorated with corriander leaves and a little grated coconut.

Papadi nu shak

250 grams thin papadis. $1\frac{1}{2}$ cups milk. $\frac{1}{4}$ coconut. A few sprigs corriander leaves. 1 small bunch corriander leaves. 2 to 3 green chillies. 1 small piece ginger. $\frac{1}{2}$ tsp. turmeric powder. $\frac{1}{2}$ tsp. garam masala. Salt to taste.

Grind ginger, chillies, coconut and the bunch of corriander to a paste. Heat 1 tblsp. ghee and fry the papadis and ground paste for 5 minutes. Put in the rest of the above ingredients with the exception of garam masala and corriander leaves. Cover and cook over a slow fire till the papadis are done. Sprinkle garam masala and corriander sprigs over top before serving.

Makkai ni Khichadi

4 corn cobs. 2 medium potatoes, boiled, peeled and mashed. 25 grams sabudana. 50 grams roasted and coarsely pounded groundnuts. 1-inch piece ginger. 3 green chillies. 2 tblsps. grated coconut. Handful of corriander leaves. A few curry leaves. Pinch of asafoetida. Sugar, salt and lime juice to taste. $\frac{1}{2}$ tsp. turmeric powder. 1 tsp. ground cumin seeds.

Soak the sabudana in water for 1 hour and then drain out the water. Grind ginger and chillies to a paste. Grate the corn and cook with very little water till tender. Mix together potatoes, corn, sabudana, groundnuts and ginger paste. Heat 2 tblsps. oil and put in the asafoetida and curry leaves, fry briefly and put in all the spices and sugar, fry for a few seconds then add the

potato mixture and fry over a gentle fire to a
light brown colour. Remove from fire and
sprinkle lime juice on top. Serve decorated
with coconut and corriander leaves.

Batata ne Tomato

250 grams baby potatoes, peeled. 100 grams tomatoes, blanched and sliced. 1-inch piece ginger
3 to 4 green chillies. A few sprigs corriander
leaves. ½ tsp. each of turmeric powder and mustard seeds. A pinch of asafoetida. 1 tsp. sugar.
Salt and chilli powder to taste.

Heat 2 tblsps. oil and toss in mustard seeds and
asafoetida, when the seeds stop popping, add
tomatoes, ground ginger and chillies and all the
spices, sugar and salt. When the tomatoes turn
soft and dry, put in the potatoes and fry for 5
minutes. Pour in 1½ cups water. Cover and
cook till the potatoes are done. Serve decorated
with sprigs of corriander leaves.

Sweet and sour potatoes

250 grams potatoes, peeled and cubed. 1 small
ball tamarind. 25 grams finely grated jaggery. ½
tsp. each of cumin and mustard seeds. 2 red chillies. 1 tsp. dhaniajeera powder. ½ tsp. turmeric
powder. A few sprigs corriander leaves. A
pinch of asafoetida. Salt and chilli powder to
taste.

Cover tamarind with water for 5 minutes and
then squeeze out the water. Put in jaggery and
set aside till it dissolves, then strain through

a muslin. Heat 3 tblsps. oil and put in asa-foetida, mustard and cumin seeds. When the seeds stop popping, put in all the spices and fry briefly, put in the potatoes and fry for 5 minutes. Pour in 2 cups water and cook till the potatoes are almost done. Now pour in the tamarind juice and continue cooking till the potatoes are soft. Serve decorated with corriander leaves.

Fried potatoes

2 big potatoes. 25 grams roasted and pounded groundnuts. 1 tblsp. roasted and pounded til. 1 tblsp. mango powder. 1 tsp. dhaniajeera powder. ¼ tsp. garam masala. Handful of sliced corriander leaves. 1 green chilli, minced. Salt and chilli powder to taste.

Peel and cut the potatoes into long fingers. Apply all the masalas nicely on potato-slices with salt. Heat 3 tblsps. oil and add the slices of potatoes, fry for 5 minutes and cover tightly and cook over a slow fire without adding water till the potatoes are done.. Mix in groundnuts and til. Serve decorated with chilli and corriander leaves.

Crunchy potatoes

3 medium potatoes. 1 tblsp. each of mango powder and dhaniajeera powder. ½ tsp. garam masala. 1 chilli, minced. 1 small green onion, finely sliced. Handful of minced corriander leaves. Salt and chilli powder to taste.

Peel and cut the potatoes into 3 to 4 pieces lengthwise. Mix together all the spices with salt. Deep fry the potatoes till they turn soft. Drain, cool and then press between your palms and press till flat, then deep fry once again till crisp and golden. Drain and mix with all spices and salt. Serve garnished with chilli, corriander leaves and onion.

Batata nu shak

250 grams potatoes, peeled and sliced. 25 grams roasted groundnuts. 50 grams roasted channa or dalia. 100 grams sour curds. 1 tsp. sugar. 1-inch piece ginger. 3 green chillies. 2 flakes garlic. 1 small piece coconut. Handful of corriander leaves. 1 big onion, finely sliced. 1 tsp. each of garam masala and dhaniajeera powder. Pinch of asafoetida. Salt and chilli powder to taste.

Grind to a paste dalia, groundnuts. Grind separately chillies, ginger, garlic, coconut and onion. Put 1 cup water in curds and beat till smooth. Heat 4 tblsps. oil and add asafoetida and ground paste and fry nicely till oil floats to the top, add all the spices and salt and fry briefly. Put in the potatoes, sugar and groundnut mixture and fry for 5 minutes. Pour in curds. Cover and cook over a slow fire till the potatoes are done. Serve decorated with corriander leaves.

Batata masala shak

500 grams potatoes, peeled and cubed. 1 tblsp.

dhaniajeera powder. $\frac{1}{2}$ tsp. turmeric powder. $\frac{1}{2}$ coconut, finely grated. 1 tsp. sugar or jaggery 1 small ball tamarind. 3 green chillies, slitted. A few sprigs corriander leaves. 1 tsp. mustard seeds. Pinch of asafoetida. Salt and chilli powder to taste.

Cover tamarind with half cup water for 5 minutes and then squeeze out the juice. Dissolve jaggery in tamarind. Heat 3 tblsps. oil and add mustard and asafoetida. When the seeds stop popping, put in all the spices and salt and fry briefly. Put in the potatoes and coconut and fry for 5 minutes. Cover potatoes with water and cook till the potatoes are almost done. Put in tamarind juice and continue cooking till the potatoes are tender and gravy thick. Serve decorated with sprigs of corriander leaves.

Potatoes in curds

500 grams baby potatoes, boiled, peeled and halved. 1 cup sour curds beaten with 1 cup water. 6 red chillies. 1 tsp. each of cumin seeds, turmeric powder and garam masala. A pinch of hing. 1 tsp. ground dry ginger. 1-inch piece ginger, minced. A few sprigs of corriander leaves. Salt to taste.

Dissolve hing and sunt or dry ginger powder in little water. Heat 2 tblsps. oil and toss in ginger red chillies and cumin seeds. When the mixture turns brown. Put in the turmeric, salt and potatoes and fry for 5 minutes, add hing water, mix nicely and then put in curds. Cook over a slow fire till the gravy turns a little thick. Serve decorated with sprigs of corriander leaves.

Masala ma batata

250 grams baby potatoes, boiled and peeled. 3 red chillies, ½ tsp. each of mustard and cumin seeds. 1-inch piece ginger, minced. 1 tblsp. dhania jeera powder. ½ tsp. garam masala. A few sprigs corriander leaves. 2 tblsps. grated coconut. Sugar, salt and lime juice to suit the taste. Pinch of asafoetida.

Heat 3 tblsps. oil and add chillies, asafoetida, mustard and cumin seeds and ginger. When the mixture turns brown, add potatoes and fry till they start changing colour. Add all the spices, salt and sugar, mix well and remove from fire. Sprinkle lime juice on top and serve decorated with coconut and corriander leaves.

Suran khichadi

500 grams suran. 25 grams roasted and pounded groundnuts. 1 tblsp. roasted and pounded til. 1 tsp. garam masala. 2 green chillies. 1 handful of corriander leaves. 1-inch piece ginger. 2 tblsps. grated coconut. Salt, sugar, lime juice and chilli powder to taste.

Peel suran and boil in water to which a little lime juice or vinegar has been added. Drain out the water and mash to a fine paste. Grind chillies, ginger and corriander leaves to a paste. Mix all the above ingredients together with the exception of lime juice, coconut and a few corriander leaves. Heat 2 tblsps. oil and fry the suran mix-

ture for 5 minutes over a slow fire. Remove
from fire sprinkle lime juice on top and decorate
with coconut and corriander leaves.

Sweet potato dabada

500 grams long and thick sweet potatoes. ¼ coconut. 1 small bunch corriander leaves. 6 green
chillies. 1 small piece ginger. 25 grams roasted
grams or dalia. A pinch asafoetida. Sugar, salt,
lime juice and chilli powder to taste. ½ tsp. turmeric powder.

Peel and cut each potato into long slices. Grind
all the above ingredients to a very smooth paste
and apply masala between two slices of potatoes.
Tie both the slices together with a piece of thread.
Heat 3 tblsps. of oil and place the potatoes side
by side in the pan. Cover tightly, sprinkle cold
water on the lid and cook without adding water
over a slow fire till the vegetable is done. You
can also bake them in a moderate oven.

Tomato shak

500 grams tomatoes, blanched and sliced. 1 clove.
1 bay leaf, crumpled. 2 cardamoms, peeled. 1
cup curds. 1 tsp. dhaniajeera powder. ¼ tsp. turmeric powder. A few sprigs corriander leaves. 3
green chillies. 1 tblsp. poppy seeds. 1-inch piece
ginger. 2 flakes garlic. 2 large onions, sliced finely.
Salt, chilli powder and sugar to taste.

Heat 3 tblsps. oil and add all the whole spices,
when they smell add the remaining spices and
fry briefly. Put the onions and fry to a golden

colour. Grind chillies, ginger, garlic and poppy seeds and mix in along with curds, salt and sugar and cook till the mixture turns dry and the oil floats to the top put in the tomato slices, sprinkle a little water on top and cook over a slow fire till the tomatoes are soft but not mushy. Serve decorated with corriander leaves.

Tomato dabada

250 grams medium tomatoes. 1 tblsp. gram flour. 1 tblsp. roasted til. $\frac{1}{4}$ coconut. 4 to 5 green chillies. 1 small bunch corriander leaves. 1 small piece ginger. 1 tsp. dhaniajeera powder. $\frac{1}{4}$ tsp. garam masala. Salt, chilli powder and sugar to taste.

Grind coconut with the rest of the above ingredients with the exception of tomatoes. Cut tops off and scoop out the inside being careful not to break the outer shells. Now mix the pulp with ground paste and fill into the tomatoes. Put the lid on and seal with flour and water paste. Heat oil and fry the tomatoes first on the sealed side nicely and then turn and fry nicely all over. Cover tightly and cook over a slow fire till the tomatoes are quite soft. Serve hot surrounded by plain boiled vegetables like carrots, beets, cauliflower, peas and french beans.

CURRIES

Bhindani curry

250 grams ladies fingers, slitted. 1 glass buttermilk. 1 tsp. gram flour. 1 tsp. turmeric powder. 1-
inch piece ginger. 4 green chillies. 1 small bunch
corriander leaves. 1 tsp. dhaniajeera powder. Salt
and chilli powder to taste. 2 flakes garlic. 1 tiny
onion. Salt to taste.

Grind ginger, chillies, corriander leaves, onion
and garlic to a paste. Mix the paste nicely with
salt and dhaniajeera powder and stuff into each
bhendi. Dissolve gram flour in buttermilk. Heat
3 tblsps. oil and fry the ladies fingers nicely, put
in the buttermilk with salt and turmeric powder
and cook over a slow fire for 10 minutes. Serve
hot with plain boiled rice.

Corn curry

4 fresh and tender corn cobs. 1 glass buttermilk.
100 grams cashewnuts. $\frac{1}{4}$ dry coconut. 2 medium
onions. 1-inch piece ginger. 2 flakes garlic 5 green
chillies. 2 medium potatoes, boiled, peeled and
cubed. 1 small bunch corriander leaves. $\frac{1}{2}$ tsp.
turmeric powder. $\frac{1}{2}$ tsp. each of garam masala
and dhaniajeera powder. Salt and chilli powder
to taste.

Roast the coconut and grind to a paste along
with ginger, garlic, chillies, cashewnuts, onions
and corriander leaves. Fry the potatoes nicely.
Remove corn from cobs. Heat 4 tblsps. ghee and
fry the ground paste till the ghee floats to the top.
Put in the cornandfry for 5 minutes, put in all
the spices and salt and mix well. Pour in the
buttermilk and cook over a slow fire till the corn
is almost done. Now add the potatoes and con-

tinue cooking till the corn is done. Serve decorated with a few sprigs of corriander leaves.

Doodhi kofta curry

2 big tomatoes. ¼ coconut. 1 tblsp. poppy seeds. 2 tblsps. curds. 10 cashewnuts. 1-inch piece ginger. 4 flakes gralic. 1 small onion. 4 green chillies. 1 small bunch corriander leaves. ½ tsp. turmeric powder. ½ tsp. each of dhaniajeera powder and garam masala. Salt, sugar and chilli powder to taste.

For koftas......500 grams pumpkin or marrow. Raisins. 2 tblsps, gram flour. 1 small bunch corriander leaves. 2 green chillies. 1 tsp. ground cumin seeds. 1 small piece ginger. A few sliced mint leaves salt and chilli powder to taste.

Peel and grate the pumpkin. Squeeze out all the moisture and set aside. Grind ginger, chillies, corriander and mint leaves coarsely. Mix with pumpkin along with all the filling ingredients with the exception of raisins. Knead the pumpkin mixture into a smooth mixture and form into small and oblong-shaped balls around a raisin. Deep fry to a golden brown colour and set aside. Grind coconut, poppy seeds, ginger, garlic and onion to a paste. Heat 3 tblsps. oil and fry the ground paste till the oil floats to the top. Put in all the spices and fry briefly. Add tomatoes, sugar and curds and cook till dry. Put in the koftas, mix well and cover with hot water. Cook over a gentle fire for 5 minutes. Serve decorated with corriander leaves.

Brinjal curry

250 grams small brinjals. 1 tsp. gram flour. 1 glass sour buttermilk. 3 green chillies, slitted. 1 tsp. cumin seeds. Handful of corriander leaves. Pinch asafoetida. ½ tsp. turmeric powder. 1 tsp. each of dhaniajeera powder and garam masala. Salt and chilli powder and sugar to taste.

Blend gram flour in buttermilk. Wash and wipe brinjals and cut into four halfway through. Mix all the spices with salt and stuff into the brinjals. Heat 4 tblsps. oil and add asafoetida and cumin seeds, when the seeds stop spluttering, put in the brinjals and fry for 5 minutes, pour in the buttermilk and cook over a slow fire till the brinjals are almost done, put in chillies and sugar and continue cooking till the brinjals are done. Serve decorated with corriander leaves.

Buttermilk curry

2 glasses of sour buttermilk. 2 tblsps. gram flour. 1 tblsp. grated jaggery. 1 tsp. dhaniajeera powder. ½ tsp. turmeric powder. A few curry leaves. ¼ tsp. each of mustard, cumin and fenugreek seeds. 1 small onion, minced. 2 flakes garlic, crushed. 1 small piece ginger, minced. 3 green chillies, slitted. 2 red chillies, broken into bits. Salt to taste.

Mix buttermilk with gram flour, salt and all the spices. Heat 2 tblsps oil and add mustard, cumin and fenugreek and red chillies and fry till the mixture turns brown. Add ginger, garlic, onion and curry leaves and cook till soft and almond coloured. Put in the buttermilk, curry leaves and the remaining ingredients and simmer gently over a slow fire for 10 minutes. Serve hot with plain boiled rice.

Mukund curry

1½ cups flour. 100 grams shelled peas. 1 large tomato, blanched and sliced. 1-inch piece ginger. 4 flakes garlic. Pinch of baking powder. 2 bay leaves. 1 glass sour buttermilk. ½ tsp. each of turmeric powder, dhaniajeera powder and garam masala. Handful of corriander leaves. 2 green chillies, slitted. 2 medium onions. Salt and chilli powder to suit the taste.

Mix together flour and salt, rub in 1 tblsp. ghee and add enough water to form a stiff dough. Wash the dough in a bowl of water till the dough turns milky white, remove the dough from water, mix in the baking powder and flatten to a thin round cake. Steam till spongy. Remove from fire, cut into small pieces and deep fry to a golden brown colour. Drain and set aside. Grind ginger, garlic and onion to a paste. Heat 2 tblsps. oil and fry the paste along with the bay leaves till the oil goes to the top. Add all spices and salt and tomatoes and cook till the tomatoes turn soft. Add peas and buttermilk and cook till the peas are done. Put in the fried pieces and chillies and cook for 5 more minutes on a gentle fire. Serve garnished with corriander leaves.

Potato kofta curry

2 small tomatoes. 250 grams beaten curds. 1 cup coconut milk. 1 tsp. turmeric powder. 1 tsp. each

of dhaniajeera powder and garam masala. 4 green chillies, slitted. 2 medium onions. 2 flakes garlic. 1 small piece ginger. Pinch of asafoetida. A few curry leaves. A few sprigs corriander leaves. Salt and chilli powder to taste.

For koftas.......2 big potatoes, boiled and peeled. 1 slice of bread, soaked in water and squeezed dry. 2 green chillies, minced. Handful of corriander leaves. 1 tsp crushed pomogranate seeds. Salt to taste. ½ tsp. turmeric powder. 50 grams gram flour. A pinch baking powder. 1 tsp. ground cumin seeds.

Mix cumin seed powder, turmeric powder, salt and baking powder in flour then add enough water to form a thick batter. Put in 1 tblsp. of hot oil and set aside for 15 minutes. Mix potatoes with chillies, bread, corriander leaves and pomogranate seeds and knead to a smooth mixture. Form the mixture into small balls, dip in batter and deep fry to a golden brown colour. Drain and set aside. Beat curds with 2 cups water till smooth. Grind ginger, garlic and onion to a paste and fry in 3 tblsps. oil till a nice brown colour. Add all the spices and salt and fry briefly. Put in tomatoes and curry leaves and cook till dry. Add coconut milk and curds and chillies and simmer over a gentle fire for 5 minutes, put in the koftas and simmer till the gravy turns a little thick. Serve garnished with corriander leaves.

Tomato curry

500 grams tomatoes, blanched and sliced. 2
cups thin and 1 cup thick coconut milk. A few
curry leaves. A few sprigs corriander leaves. $\frac{1}{2}$
tsp. each of turmeric and dhaniajeera powder and
garam masala. 1 small piece ginger. 2 flakes garlic.
1 medium onion. 4 green chillies,, slitted. Pinch
of asafoetida. 1 tblsp. gram flour. $\frac{1}{4}$ tsp. each of
mustard and cumin seeds. Salt and sugar to taste.
Grind onion, ginger and garlic to a paste. Blend
gram flour in thin coconut milk. Heat 3 tblsps.
oil and add asafoetida, mustard and cumin seeds,
when the seeds stop spluttering, add the ground
paste and fry nicely, put in tomatoes, curry leaves.
all the spices, salt and sugar and cook till dry.
Put thin coconut milk and chillies. When the
curry turns a little thick, pour in the thick coconut milk and remove from fire. Sprinkle corriander leaves on top before serving with plain boiled
rice.

DALS

Mixed dal

½ cup each of toovar, moong and urad dal, 1 brinjal, cubed. 2 drumsticks, scraped and cut into pieces. 4 green chillies, slitted, 2 large tomatoes, blanched and diced. A few curry leaves. A handful of corriander leaves. 1-inch piece ginger, minced. ½ tsp. turmeric powder. A big pinch asafoetida. ½ tsp. each of cumin and mustard seeds. 1 tsp. sugar. Salt to taste.

Wash and soak the dals in water for 1 hour, then drain out the water. Heat 2 tblsps. oil and add ginger, when it turns soft, add the dals and turmeric. Cover with water and cook till the dals turn soft. Remove from fire, mash to a paste and pass through a sieve. Heat 2 tblsps. ghee and put in tomatoes and salt, cook till the tomatoes turn soft. Put in vegetables and ½ tsp. garam masala, curry leaves, sugar and chillies and fry for 5 minutes, put in 3 cups water and the dals. Cover and cook till the vegetables are done— Remove from fire and set aside. Heat 1 tblsp. ghee and put in the mustard and cumin seeds and asafoetida. When the seeds stop popping, put into the dal. Serve with plain boiled rice.

Radish in dal

1 cup moong dal. 2 big tender radishes. 1 tsp. cumin seeds. ½ tsp. turmeric powder. 1 small ball tamarind. A pinch asafoetida. Salt and chilli powder to taste. 1-inch piece ginger, minced.

Cover tamarind with water for 5 minutes and squeeze out the juice. Wash and soak dal in water for 1 hour, then cook in the water in which it was soaked after adding to it turmeric powder till it is half done. Peel and cut radishes into small pieces. Also mince the tender leaves of raddishes and put into the half cooked dal. Cook till the dal and the vegetables are almost done. Put in tamarind, salt and chilli powder and continue cooking till done. Remove from fire and set aside. Heat 2 tblsps. oil and toss in asafoetida, cumin seeds and ginger. When the seeds stop popping, put over the dal. Serve with plain boiled rice.

Vegetable dal

2 cups toovar dal. 1 small ball tamrind. 2 tblsps. grated jaggery. 4 green chillies, slitted. A few cauliflower flowerets. 10 baby potatoes peeled. 50 grams peeled and diced pumpkin. 50 grams peeled and diced and boiled suran. 1 medium tomato, peeled and sliced. A few curry leaves. $\frac{1}{2}$ tsp. turmeric powder. 1 tsp. cumin seeds. 6 flakes garlic. 1-inch piece ginger, sliced. 1 small piece coconut, sliced. 25 grams cashewnuts. Handful of sliced corriander leaves. Salt to taste.

Boil dal along with turmeric powder till soft. Remove from fire, pass through a sieve after mashing it. Put in 3 cups hot water. Cover tamarind with 1 cup water for 5 minutes and then squeeze out the water. Dissolve jaggery in tamarind water. Heat 2 tblsps. ghee and fry the vegetables with the exception of suran along with curry leaves cashewnuts and chillies for 5 minutes. Put in the dal and cook till the vegetables are almost done. Put in the suran and tamarind and corriander leaves and continue cooking till the vegetables are done. Remove from fire and set aside. Heat

2 tblsps. ghee and put in cumin seeds, ginger and garlic. When the mixture turns brown put it over the dal. Serve decorated with coconut.

Pumpkin dal

250 grams toovar dal. 250 grams pumpkin, peeled and sliced. 1 big tomato, blanched and sliced. 1 small onion, finely sliced. 2 green and 2 fresh red chillies, minced. ¼ tsp. each of mustard and cumin seeds. A pinch asafoetida. A few sprigs corriander leaves. ½ tsp. turmeric powder. ¼ coconut, finely grated. 1 tsp. fenugreek seeds. Salt to taste.

Fry the fenugreek seeds to a red colour and powder. Heat 2 tblsps. ghee and add onion and fry till soft. Put in the washed dal along with turmeric and 4 cups water. Cook till the dal turns soft. Remove from fire, mash to a paste and pass through a sieve. Heat 1 tblsp. ghee and cook the tomatoes till soft. Put in the pumpkin, powdered fenugreek seeds, salt and ground coconut and fry for 5 minutes. Put in the dal along with 3 cups water and chillies and cook till the vegetable turns soft. Remove from fire and set aside. Heat 1 tblsp. ghee and add asafoetida, ginger and mustard and cumin seeds. When the seeds stop popping, put into the dal. Serve decorated with corriander leaves.

Dal with sweet potatoes

1 cup toovar dal. 2 medium sweet potatoes, peeled and sliced. ½ tsp. turmeric powder. 1-inch piece ginger, minced. 3 green chillies, minced. A few

sprigs corriander leaves. 1 small ball tamarind. A pinch asafoetida. 1 tsp. grated jaggery. 1 small ball tamarind. Salt to taste. 1 tsp. cumin seeds.

Cover tamarind with half cup water for 5 minutes and then squeeze out the juice. Wash and soak dal in water for 1 hour and then boil in the water in which it was soaked till soft. Remove from fire. Mash to a pulp and pass through a sieve. Dissolve jaggery in tamarind. Put sweet potatoes in dal, add turmeric, salt and 2 cups water and cook till the potatoes turn soft. Mash the potatoes coarsely and put in the tamarind. Cook for 5 more minutes and remove from fire. Heat 1 tblsp. ghee and put in asafoetida and cumin seeds. When the seeds stop popping, put in the chillies and ginger and fry till soft. Put over the dal. Serve decorated with corriander leaves.

Dal moong

1 cup moong dal with skins. 4 green chillies, minced. 1 big piece ginger, minced. 6 flakes garlic, crushed lightly. 1 tsp. cumin seeds. A pinch of asafoetida. ½ tsp. turmeric powder. Salt to suit the taste.

Wash and soak the dal in water for 1 hour. Heat 1 tblsp. oil and fry ginger and chillies lightly. Put in the dal along with the water in which it was soaked and turmeric powder and cook till the dal is almost done. Put in salt and continue cooking till the dal turns soft. Remove from fire and set aside. Heat 2 tblsps. ghee and toss in asafoetida, cumin seeds and garlic. When the mixture starts changing colour, put into the dal.

Dal toovar

2 cups toovar dal. 6 cleaned and washed cocums. 1 tblsp. grated jaggery. 4 green chillies, minced. 1 tsp. ground cumin seeds. $\frac{1}{2}$ tsp. turmeric powder. 1 tblsp. corriander powder. $\frac{1}{4}$ tsp. garam masala. A few sprigs corriander leaves. Salt and chilli powder to taste.

Wash and soak the dal in water for 1 hour. Then put it to boil along with the water in which it was soaked after adding to it turmeric powder till soft. Remove from fire, mash and pass through a sieve. Clean and wash the cocums. Put the cocums into the dal along with the rest of the above ingredients with the exception of corriander leaves and mix well. Put in 1 cup water and boil for 10 minutes. Remove from fire and decorate with corriander leaves.

Toovar dal No. 2.

1 cup of toovar dal. 1 small ball tamarind. 1 tsp. grated jaggery. A pinch asafoetida. $\frac{1}{2}$ tsp. mustard seeds. 1-inch piece ginger, minced. 4 green chillies, minced. $\frac{1}{2}$ tsp. turmeric powder. Salt and chilli powder to taste.

Wash and soak dal in water for 1 hour. Put the dal to cook along with the water in which it was soaked till it turns soft. Remove from fire, mash and pass through a sieve. Cover tamarind with water for 5 minutes and squeeze out the juice. Put tamarind, jaggery, ginger, chillies and salt in dal along with 2 cups water and boil for 10 minutes. Remove from fire and set aside. Heat 2 tblsps. ghee and add asafoetida cumin seeds and 1 tsp. chilli powder. When the seeds stop popping, put over the dal. Serve decorated with sprigs of corriander leaves.

Sukhe val

1 cup sukhe or dry val. 4 raw bananas, peeled and sliced. 2 green and 2 fresh red chillies, minced. A pinch of asafoetida. ½ cup curds. 1 tsp. sugar. ½ tsp. turmeric powder. Handful of sliced corriander leaves. ½ tsp. ground cumin seeds. ½ tsp. garam masala. Salt and chilli powder to taste. 1-inch piece ginger, minced.

Soak val whole night in water. Next morning, boil them in the water in which they were soaked till soft. Remove from fire and set aside. Heat 2 tblsps. oil and add chillies, asafoetida and ginger. When the mixture turns soft. Add all the spices and fry briefly. Put in the bananas and salt and fry for 5 minutes. Put in the curds, cover tightly and cook till the bananas are almost cooked, put in the sugar and cooked val and continue cooking till the bananas are done. Serve garnished with corriander leaves.

Savoury peas

1 cup dried peas, ¼ coconut. 1 small onion. 1-inch piece ginger. 1 tsp. garam masala. 1 tblsp. corriander powder. 1 tsp. ground cumin seeds. ½ tsp. turmeric powder. Pinch of sugar. 2 medium tomatoes, blanched and sliced. A few sprigs corriander leaves. 4 green chillies, slitted. 1 sour lime,

cut into thin wedges. Salt to suit the taste. 1 tsp. mustard seeds. Salt and chilli powder to taste.

Soak peas in water whole night. Next morning, drain out the water and tie in a piece of cloth and set aside for 24 hours at the end of which the peas will develop sprouts. Brown onion and coconut in a little ghee and grind it to a thick paste. Heat 3 tblsps. oil and add ginger and tomatoes, when the tomatoes turn soft. Add all the spices, salt and peas. Mix well, cover with water and cook till the peas are almost done. Put in the ground coconut paste and sugar and continue cooking till the peas are done and the gravy quite thick. Remove from fire and put in a serving dish. Heat 2 tblsps. ghee and put in a pinch of asafoetida and mustard seeds. When the seeds stop popping, put over the peas. Decorate with chillies, corriander leaves and wedges of lime before serving.

Dal with spinach

2 bunches spinach. 125 grams moong dal without skins. 4 green chillies, minced. 1-inch piece ginger, minced. $\frac{1}{2}$ tsp. turmeric powder. $\frac{1}{2}$ tsp. garam masala. 2 firm and red tomatoes, cut into thin rings. Potato straws. Salt and chilli powder to taste.

Clean and wash the spinach. Cut finely and put in ginger and chillies and salt and cook without adding water till tender. Remove from fire and keep it warm. Wash and soak dal in water for 1 hour. Cook in the water in which it was soaked after adding to it salt, turmeric powder

and garam masala till tender and completly dry.
Take a dish and cover the bottom with spinach,
place dal over the spinach in a even layer and
put rings of tomatoes over top. Sprinkle chilli
powder and potato straws over top before serving. This is a very nutritious and delicious dish.

Toovar dal treat

250 grams toovar dal. 50 grams urad dal. 100
grams suran. 25 grams raw groundnuts. 4 green
chillies, slitted. 2 drumsticks, scraped and cut
into 2-inch pieces. 1-inch piece ginger, minced.
Handful of corriander leaves. 1 lime-sized ball
of tamarind. 1 tblsp. grated jaggery. ½ tsp. mustard seeds. Pinch of asafoetida. Salt to taste.

Soak groundnuts in water for half an hour, drain
and remove peels. Soak urad dal whole night in
water. Next morning, drain and grind to a
coarse paste and fry in little oil to a nice red
colour. Cover tamrind in water for 5 minutes
and then squeeze out the pulp. Wash and soak
toovar dal in water for 1 hour. Then boil in
water in which it was soaked after adding to it
½ tsp. turmeric powder. Remove from fire, mash
and pass through a sieve. Put in vegetables and
peanuts or groundnuts and put on fire. Add as
much water as you like for gravy. Cook till the
vegetables turn almost tender, then mix in the
rest of the above ingredients with the exception
of corriander leaves, ginger, mustard and asafoetida. When the vegetables are done, remove
from fire and set aside. Heat 2 tblsps. oil and
add asafoetida, mustard and ginger, when the

seeds stop popping, put over the dal. Sprinkle corriander leaves on top before serving.

Dal kofta curry

250 grams baby potatoes, boiled and peeled. 2 medium onions. 1-inch piece ginger. 2 big tomatoes, blanched and sliced. 4 green chillies, slitted. 4 flakes garlic. A few sprigs corriander leaves. 2 cups coconut milk. ½ tsp. turmeric powder. 1 tsp. garam masala. Salt and chilli powder to taste.

For koftas......1 cup channa dal. 1 small onion. minced. 1 small piece ginger, minced. 1 tblsp. grated coconut. A few raisins. Handful of minced corriander leaves. Salt to taste.

Soak dal whole night in water. Next morning, drain out the water nicely and grind to a paste. Mix in all the kofta ingredients with the exception of raisins. Form the mixture into small balls around a raisin and deep fry to a golden colour. Drain and set aside. Grind onion, ginger and garlic to a paste. Heat 3 tblsps. oil and fry the ground paste nicely. Put in all the spices and salt and cook till the tomatoes turn soft. Put in the potatoes and fry for 5 minutes. Pour in coconut milk and bring slowly to a boil, reduce heat and toss in the koftas, simmer gently for 5 minutes and remove from fire. Serve decorated with corriander leaves.

Moong curry

100 grams whole moong. 1 glass butter milk. 1 tblsp. gram flour. ½ tsp. cumin seeds. 1 tsp. sugar. 4 green chillies, slitted. 1 smal piece ginger, minced. A few curry leaves. Handful of corriander leaves. ½ tsp. turmeric powder. Pinch asafoetida. Salt to taste.

Wash and soak dal in water whole night. Next morning, tie in a cloth and hang from a nail in the wall for 24 hours at the end of which the dal will have developed sprouts. Mix flour with buttermilk. Heat 2 tblsps. oil and add asafoetida, cumin seeds and ginger. When the seeds stop popping, put in dal and turmeric powder and salt. Pour in 1 cup water and curry leaves and cook till the dal is almost done. Pour in buttermilk and add chillies and sugar and cook till the dal is soft. Garnish with corriander leaves and serve with plain boiled rice.